World Youth Day 1992

Live the Faith, Share the Story!

Secretariat for Family, Laity, Women and Youth
National Conference of Catholic Bishops

In September 1988, the Administrative Committee of the National Conference of Catholic Bishops approved a request that World Youth Day be observed in the United States on the Thirtieth Sunday in Ordinary Time. Accordingly, in its planning document, as approved by the general membership of the National Conference of Catholic Bishops in November 1991, the Secretariat for Family, Laity, Women and Youth was authorized to produce a World Youth Day manual. This present document, *Live the Faith, Share the Story!* was prepared by Mr. Paul Henderson, associate director, in consultation with the staff of the Secretariat for Family, Laity, Women and Youth. The text has been reviewed and approved by Mrs. Dolores R. Leckey, executive director of the secretariat, and is authorized for publication by the undersigned.

Monsignor Robert N. Lynch
General Secretary
NCCB/USCC

April 20, 1992

Cover Photograph by Arturo Mari, *L'Osservatore Romano*; Citta del Vaticano. American youths receive the International Youth Cross from their Polish peers in a symbolic exchange that heralds the site of the next International World Youth Day Celebration to be held in Denver, Colorado, in 1993.

Text Illustrations: Ted Jarkiewicz Studio; Baltimore, Maryland

Photographs on pp. 12, 14, 17, 19, and 42 (English) and pp. 2, 5, and 8 (Spanish) by Jim Whitmer; Wheaton, Illinois. Photographs on pp. 4 and 33 by Michael Hoyt/Catholic Standard; Washington, D.C. Photographs on pp. 24 and 26 by CNS/Crosiers; Washington, D.C. Used with permission. All rights reserved.

ISBN 1-55586-499-6

Acknowledgments

Special thanks are extended to the 1992 World Youth Day Planning Committee and to the members of the NCCB/USCC Task Force on Youth and Young Adult Ministry for their assistance in the development of the theme and selection of authors for this manual: Ms. Beverly Carroll, NCCB Secretariat for Black Catholics; Ms. Susan Stolfa, USCC Campaign for Human Development; Sr. Elaine McCarron, USCC Department of Education; Mr. Ron Cruz, NCCB Secretariat for Hispanic Affairs; Mr. Paul Henderson, NCCB Secretariat for Family, Laity, Women and Youth; Ms. Marie Quinlan, USCC Office for the Pastoral Care of Migrants and Refugees; Ms. Nancy Wisdo, USCC Department of Social Development and World Peace; Fr. Len Wenke, National Federation for Catholic Youth Ministry; Mr. Wayne Smith, National Catholic Educational Association and Mr. Neil Parent, National Conference of Catechetical Leadership.

Thanks are also extended to the authors of the essays contained in this book; to the Bishops' Committee on the Laity for its support of young people generally and for this project in particular; to the staff of the Secretariat for Family, Laity, Women and Youth for the review of the manual, especially Mr. Paul Henderson, who coordinated the project; Ms. Bonnie Stallings, secretary; and to the USCC Office for Publishing and Promotion Services for its assistance in publishing this manual.

May 1992 be a year for all of us to renew our commitment to the pastoral care and physical well-being of children and youths around the world.

Dolores R. Leckey, Executive Director
Secretariat for Family, Laity, Women and Youth
National Conference of Catholic Bishops

Contents

A Brief History

World Youth Day has its beginnings in the year 1985 with the observance of the United Nations International Year of the Youth. At this time, the Holy Father, in observance of the U. N. celebration, invited young people from around the world to meet with him on Palm Sunday in Rome for fellowship, catechesis, and worship.

That year many youths from the United States joined young people from around the world in Rome to celebrate their faith and their youthfulness. Few realized that this marked the beginning of a wonderful tradition.

For the Holy Father, his meeting with young people and his special letter to them was to continue beyond the U.N. observance and become a yearly celebration. Since 1985, John Paul II has issued a letter addressed to the youths of the world, and on alternating years (1985, 1987, 1989, and 1991) he has invited the youths of the world to meet with him at one location for catechesis, fellowship, worship, and renewal. These meetings have now taken place in Rome, Buenos Aires, Santiago de Compostela, and Czestochowa, respectively. The next meeting is planned for 1993.

In the United States, our national celebration of World Youth Day has been developing slowly. At first, with the yearly observance held on Palm Sunday, the event was primarily a Mass with the bishop in the cathedral. In 1988, for pastoral considerations, the Administrative Committee of the National Conference of Catholic Bishops chose a different date for the U.S. celebration to allow more parishes and schools to participate and so as not to conflict with Palm Sunday and preparations for the Triduum and Easter Sunday. After consultation with the NCCB Secretariat for the Liturgy, the Thirtieth Sunday in Ordinary Time was selected. This is typically the last Sunday of October. The date was chosen because of the appropriateness of the lectionary readings and because it would not conflict with other national celebrations and observances.

The Celebration

In the United States, our celebration of World Youth Day has focused primarily on adolescents—those in junior high and high school—while in Europe and in many other parts of the world, it is primarily a day of celebration and commemoration for college students and young adults. As this celebration grows in its acceptance and practice in the United States, we invite college students and young adults to join in World Youth Day activities and to make this day their own!

> Young people are not a church by themselves. They are members of an intergenerational community. . . . World Youth Day is a celebration of the Church's youthfulness!

Today, World Youth Day is predominately observed on the Thirtieth Sunday of Ordinary Time, with some dioceses having celebrations on Palm Sunday, which typically initiate yearlong observances that conclude with parish and school activities at the end of October. No matter when it is celebrated, it is most important that it be celebrated in the dioceses, in our parishes, and in our schools!

Today, more than ever, young people need the support and affirmation of parents and the local community. Last January, the bishops of the United States released a message asking all Catholics, all people—families, churches, schools, governments— to place children and youths first in time, resources, and energy. World

Youth Day can be a day to raise up our young people, to affirm their talents and gifts, to welcome them and their participation in our lives and that of our institutions.

Four Perspectives

This booklet is designed to assist diocesan, parish, school, and other youth leaders in developing programs and activities for World Youth Day 1992. We further suggest, where possible, that parishes and schools use the theme during the 1992-1993 school year. Also, consider linking the theme with national and ecclesial holidays.

In your planning, we ask you to consider *four perspectives* that we hope will make World Youth Day a better celebration.

1. Family

Make certain that activities and liturgies involve the whole family and build up the family as the primary way of passing on our faith.

2. Multicultural

Plan so that activities and liturgies reflect the cultural mix of the community, both ecclesial (parish and school) and civic.

3. Global

Keep in mind when planning activities and worship that World Youth Day is a celebration of youths throughout the world. This day should challenge us to remember the lived experience of young people around the globe.

4. Intergenerational

Consider that activities for World Youth Day not only involve youth groups, religious education, school and scouting programs but the entire parish community.

Young people are not a church by themselves. They are members of an intergenerational community. Young people can, and should, participate alongside children and adults in the life of the parish church. World Youth Day is not just a celebration for teens but for the whole parish and the whole school community (including parents). World Youth Day is a celebration of the Church's youthfulness!

Speaking of his meeting with over 1 million youths in Czestochowa, Poland, the Holy Father says:

> Once again the world was able to see the Church, so young and so missionary, full of joy and hope . . . a new step on the road of evangelization . . . a new Pentecost . . . youths are the protagonists (John Paul II, *Address to Youth, 1992*).

Reflecting on the Theme

Live the Faith, Share the Story!

Attitude! We all have one! Attitude reflects what we think about ourselves, our world, and our fellow human beings. How we approach God is also based on our attitude. Each of the readings for World Youth Day (Sunday) speaks of different attitudes.

In the Sirach reading, we are told of God's attitude: he hears the cry of the poor . . . he knows no favorites . . . those who approach God in humility, their prayers reach the heavens. Paul's attitude in 2 Timothy is one of confidence because the Lord is with him—he has done his job: "I have finished the race. . . . I have kept the faith. . . ."

The gospel reading paints two contrasting attitudes. The Pharisee who proudly boasts of his justification before God as a result of his good deeds and the tax collector who, recognizing his faults, comes before God in humility, seeking mercy. This passage further reminds us that our attitude and that of society may not always be that of Christ; that what we often think is the way to holiness is not; that what we loudly proclaim to be the best way or the only way is not.

The challenge is to be open to God's presence in new ways of thinking and acting and in new experiences; that through those who we feel are the least we are taught the most. What is our attitude toward our God and our faith?

The 1992 celebration of World Youth Day presents us with an opportunity to reflect on our attitude toward God, his people, and our faith. 1992 challenges us to understand our Christian heritage, to put on the attitude of Christ, and to share the Christian story! Again, what is our attitude toward our faith? Do we keep it hidden and to ourselves, a private personal experience? Or do we bring it out into the open and let it shine forth for others to see? Living our faith demands the sharing of the message, since what we hold as a value is never kept a secret but is always shared with others.

In his message to the youths of the world in 1990, the Holy Father challenged young people to examine their attitude toward their faith.

He asked them to be the new apostles for the next decade. Today, in 1992, John Paul II again challenges our attitude. He asks youths to realize that they have much to give to the Church and to society:

You must have the courage to speak about Christ to your families and in your environment of study, work or recreation. The energy and enthusiasm which you, dear young people, can offer the Church are indispensable. To be disciples of Christ is not a private fact . . . on the contrary, the gift of faith must be shared with others.

> Living our faith demands the sharing of the message, since what we hold as a value is never kept a secret but is always shared with others.

The Holy Father further says that youths are called to be missionaries now among their family and friends:

Young Catholics are called to show through their lifestyles and decisions that belief is a credible alternative to indifference or even hostility. Christians, no matter what their age, must have the courage to "propose Christ" to everyone searching for meaning in their lives. Go out into the whole world and proclaim the Good News.

Put on the attitude of Christ!

In other words, the Holy Father challenges young people to action! They are challenged to live the faith and share the story.

Live the Faith

"Put on" the attitude of Christ! What is the attitude of Christ? It is one of humility, mercy, and care for God's creation. The sin of the Pharisee in the gospel is that he came trusting his own goodness and righteousness rather than placing himself before God and relying on God's forgiveness and mercy. The Pharisee could do it all himself. He did not need God's forgiveness or God's help. 1992 presents us with an opportunity to reflect on our own need for God's mercy and forgiveness in ways we have acted both individually and as a people: in our treatment of the environment; in our treatment of those who are powerless; in our treatment of our children and youths. This attitude of humility is also a recognition of the need to "put on" the attitude of Christ.

Share the Story

Be evangelizers to family, friends, and society. Youths as initiated members of the community are called to be signs of God's loving presence in this world. While traditional wisdom has painted young people as recipients of adult wisdom—"When teens grow up they then are able to add something to Church and society—youths are able to contribute as adolescents to our communities. Young people can take up the challenge of being instruments of God in their world: in the family, in the schoolyard, at work, and at church. Young people have a special call to be signs of Christ's love, especially among other young people. Adults can listen and learn from young people, and those who have worked with youths testify to this. We walk our faith journey together, each person respecting, giving, and receiving from one another.

Paul K. Henderson
Associate Director
Secretariat for Family, Laity,
Women and Youth
National Conference of
Catholic Bishops
Washington, D.C.

A Blueprint for Celebrating World Youth Day

The Importance of Planning Your Celebration

Celebrating World Youth Day in the parish or in the school presents an opportunity to focus the attention and prayers of the community on the valuable gifts of young people. It is an opportunity for the community to reflect on the role of young people and to be challenged to be fully inclusive of youths.

It is the right moment for youths, likewise, to reflect on their own gifts and presence to the faith community. With a little bit of advance planning, many of the elements of this manual can be integrated into already existing parish youth ministry or school programming.

What follows is a blueprint for a parish or a school celebration of World Youth Day 1992. Included is a sample process for getting started as well as a plan of action using elements of this manual. This blueprint is meant to serve as a practical guide. Adjustment and adaptation may be necessary, depending on the resources and needs unique to each parish or school.

Getting Started Early Summer

The "Dream Stage"

Read *Live the Faith, Share the Story!* from cover to cover. Live to share the spirit of this year's theme. Questions to ask:

- What will work in this setting? What will not work?

- What is unique about this community and its young people with regard to the theme (e.g., vibrant multiethnic community, strong ecumenical focus, parish actively involved in the local secular community, full-inclusion of persons with disabilities)?

- What is it about the individual and collective histories of this community that names our Christian story?

Who Needs to Know?

Identify key leadership in the parish/school and inform them of World Youth Day.

- First, compile a contact list of leadership with whom the date, theme, and possible celebration ideas need to be shared. These are the people who will become partners in advocating that a World Youth Day celebration happens in the community. Include the pastoral ministry staff, parish council, youth ministry core team, and other parish leadership whose work impacts or is impacted by youth.

- Second, send the background information about World Youth Day to the people on the list. In addition to the date for this year's celebration, be sure to include the following from this year's manual, *Live the Faith, Share the Story!:* the articles "Reflecting on the Theme" and "Integrating Youth into the Parish"; selected Reproducible Art" relative to this year's theme; and John Paul II's "Message to the Youth of the World."

- Third, place the topic "World Youth Day 1992—Our Parish/School Celebration" on the meeting agendas of the parish ministry staff, the parish council, the youth ministry core team, and any other applicable groups. Items to cover are the following: a brief history of the origin of World Youth Day and its importance in the life of the universal and local Church (see "Getting Started"); the theme for 1992 (see "Reflecting on the Theme"); the date for the celebration in the United States (October 25, 1992); and a proposed plan of action (e.g., the plan that follows).

Planning Ahead Late Summer

Setting a Goal

Enable youth and adult volunteers to begin the planning and preparation for implementing a World Youth Day celebration. For schools, this step can be taken at the start of the school year so long as the events have been calendared previously.

Please note, if the parish or school is culturally diverse, multicultural representation and participation are a given. The celebration is meant to reflect truly the heritage, challenges, and hopes of the entire community. With this planning team, develop the goal and objectives for the community's World Youth Day celebration. Ask yourselves: "What do we want to accomplish and how?"

Advance Publicity

Begin advance publicity, using these and other techniques geared toward your community:

- Share the theme of World Youth Day in creative ways. Focus the community on young people and their role as related to the celebration's theme. For example, collect stories that reflect the heritage of mission and action. Title the project "(Name of Your Community): Sharing the Story of Christ." Coordinate interviews to let others hear the stories. Who is, or has been, a young person with a story to share about mission and action? In what ways

have members of the community "lived the faith?" Ask older parishioners to share their stories of mission and action from when they were young. Ask youths to share their own stories, as the youths who contributed to the section "Stories of Young People" in this manual.

Tap into the richness of the community's Christian heritage, with particular attention to the unique cultural and ethnic expressions of that heritage. For example, listen to and share with others the stories of first-generation Hispanic youths and adults, of young Vietnamese refugees, of Eastern European youths, of African American youths in the community.

- Publish excerpts from these stories in the weekly parish bulletin during the summer months or in the first issue of the school newsletter.

- Devote a small space in the weekly parish bulletin to information related to World Youth Day. Use this manual as a resource. Possible options are to print the "Refelction on the Theme," some history of World Youth Day (from "Getting Started"), or one of the "Stories of Young People."

- Send out teams—try youths paired with adults—to interview parishioners. Produce a documenatry of the community's Christian heritage by videotaping families and youths sharing their stories.

- Feature individual youth, adult, and the community stories on a bulletin board in the gathering place of the parish or the school. Include pictures and excerpts from the stories. Illustrate how members of the youth community (past and present) have lived the faith and "put on the attitude of Christ."

Keeping a Schedule

Mark on your calendar the dates for all activities planned for the celebration of World Youth Day. In addition to the dates for the actual events, carefully determine the specifics of any pre-event planning. For example, if the "One-Day Retreat" is chosen, schedule team preparation, facility use, and so forth.

Sample Schedule

OCTOBER 1991
World Youth Day Scripture Journal

- Develop a simple journal that includes scripture reflections based on the readings for World Youth Day 1992; reflections on John Paul II's *Message to the Youth of the World*; reflections on the theme; and voices of the community.

- Use this journal as a catechetical tool during the month of October. Or, extend the celebration of World Youth Day into November by offering this journal for use after World Youth Day.

OCTOBER 17, 1992
One-Day Retreat

- Develop a one-day retreat, using the model presented in this manual as a basis. Adapt as needed to fit your community.

OCTOBER 21, 1992
Adult Learning Session

- Develop an adult learning session, using the model presented in this manual as a basis. Adapt as needed to fit your community.

OCTOBER 24, 1992
Prayer Vigil/Reconciliation Service

- Use the Prayer Service for World Youth Day 1992 in the section on "Suggestions for Prayer and Worship." When planning the Prayer Vigil, consider the importance of cultural symbols, rituals, and traditions to the community's faith expression. Use music, art, and movement that will call the young people of the community to prayer, reflection, and challenge. Invite the families of the young people to participate.

OCTOBER 25, 1992
Liturgical Celebration

- Determine the schedule for this liturgy in collaboration with the pastoral staff, the liturgy committee, and the young people of the community. Use the liturgy in the "Suggestions for Prayer and Worship" section in this manual as a guide.

OCTOBER 25, 1992
Gathering the Community

- Invite the entire community to an evening celebration. The following suggestions are offered here, but be creative and make the celebration your own.

  - **Presentation: "Putting on the Attitude."** Use skits, videotapes, slides, singing, and stories that share how the youths of the community have put on the attitude of Christ. Use this opportunity to share with the community the stories gathered during the summer.

  - **Shared Meal.** Involve parish organizations in coordinating food stations reflective of the cultures in the community (e.g., African American, Asian, Cuban, German, Italian, Mexican, Native American, Polish). Perhaps, a group of ethnically diverse young people will want to contribute a food station reflecting the youth culture. The process of planning and sharing a meal can be a powerful intergenerational experience for youths.

  - **Small-Group Process.** Provide a forum for follow-up within the large-group gathering for the participants on the "One-Day Retreat," the "Adult Learning Session," and other events.

  - **Motivational Witness and Challenge Talk.** Listen to youths challenge the community. Listen to the community challenge its young people. See the section on "Stories of Young People" for examples of these challenges.

More Suggestions

For parishes and schools with limited staff and volunteers, a simpler way of celebrating World Youth Day might include the following:

- **Sunday Mass.** Have one of the regularly scheduled Masses include a celebration of World Youth Day. Involve both young people and their families.

- **Reception.** Have the Parish Council, the PTA, the Holy Name Society, or another adult-membership organization sponsor and host a reception for the young people after Mass. Honor one or two youths who have contributed to the parish or community by recognizing their gifts and talents.

Some other ways parishes and schools have marked previous World Youth Day celebrations include the following:

- Rosary Rally
- Weekend Retreat
- Service Project
- School Rally and Mass (on a Friday)

- Pilgrimage of Diocesan Youths (or Several Parishes)
- Youth Conference or Forum
- Youth Participation in Liturgical Roles at All Masses
- Reflections after Communion.

By using imagination and creativity, you can make your parish and school celebrations unique and inspirational for all members of the community—both young and old, as together, you "Live the Faith, Share the Story!"

Assessing the Celebration

Refer to the specific goal and objectives decided upon in the initial planning process to assess the community's World Youth Day celebration. Last year's manual, *Seeing with New Eyes, Acting in Solidarity,* offers an explanation and some examples of the Pastoral Circle Model: involvement, exploration, reflection, and action (see pp. 13-16), which could be used as a guide for your assessment.

Continuing the Celebration

World Youth Day does not have to end abruptly on October 25, 1992. Review the parish and school activities found in this manual. Those ideas that are not used as a part of the specific focus of the community's celebration, may be appropriate in the overall schema of the total year's emphasis. Consider this manual and its contents as resource materials and program ideas for the evangelizing efforts that are part of the total youth ministry thrust throughout the year.

Susan B. Stark , Director
Office of Youth /Young Adult Ministries
Diocese of San Diego

Sharing the Christian Story

Plan a "Celebration of the Saints" from the many cultures that make up our Church. This celebration would be prepared by the young people of the parish.

It would consist of a reception, either in the parish hall or in an outdoors area, with a table set up for each of the cultures. Each table could include the following elements:

- a shrine for a saint from the particular cultural community;
- a picture or statue of the saint;
- a poster describing the life of the saint and the way in which he or she lived the life of Christ;
- information about the culture of the saint (e.g., maps, values of the community, pictures of families, stories of migration to the United States);
- cookies, bread, or snacks from the culture.

Following a World Day of Youth Liturgy, parishioners would be invited to participate in this celebration and discover the wide variety of people from around the world who have lived their faith and shared the story of Christ!

Prayer for Youths

Invite the parish community to pray for the youths of the world by distributing prayer cards and asking each person to pray at a designated time each day during the week before World Youth Day.

- **Step 1:** Invite the youths of the community to design art and graphics for the prayer card, and then have the card printed.

- **Step 2:** Distribute the prayer card to the parish community on the Sunday before World Youth Day. Have the presider or the commentator explain the card and the prayer request. Accompany this request with an announcement in the bulletin, such as the following:

You are invited to pray for the youths of the world. Pope John Paul II and leaders of our universal Church have set aside next Sunday as World Youth Day. The theme for this year is "Live the Faith, Share the Story!" This Sunday, prayer cards will be distributed. We are asked to pray for all the youths of the world this week at 6:00 p.m. each day. You may pray on your own or gather with family, friends, or co-workers for this special prayer.

- **Step 3:** During the celebration of World Youth Day, include a thank-you to all the parishioners who have prayed for the youths. Incorporate the prayer in the Sunday liturgy, and invite the community to continue to pray for the youths in special ways throughout the year.

The following, or a similar, text may be used for the prayer card:

World Youth Day 1992
Live the Faith, Share the Story!

Loving Creator God,
  we pray in solidarity with your
  people throughout the world for
  the youths.
Bless them today with safety
  from violence, drugs, poverty,
  and self-destruction.
Increase within them the Spirit of
Christ
  to become signs of your love,
  and leaders in hope, for justice
  and peace.
Unite them, with all of your creation, in a song of love to you
  in thanksgiving for the wondrous gift of life.
We ask this through Christ our
Lord. Amen.

Lectionary-based Scripture Sharing

Develop a scripture study for young people using the Gospels for the four Sundays of October. This faith sharing could be part of another program or it could be a specially offered program. Plan for about one hour and fifteen minutes of sharing and community building each week. The sharing should be scheduled sometime during the week before the Gospel will be read as part of the Sunday liturgy. Keep the study and reflection simple in design:

Welcome/Reflection

Question/Shared Prayer

First Reading of Gospel
- ◆ What do you hear?
- ◆ What is the one word or phrase that stands out for you?
- ◆ How does this reading make you feel?

Second Reading of Gospel
Share research and reflection about the meaning of the passage. (You could ask parish clergy for a commentary on the Scriptures.)
- ◆ What is Jesus telling his disciples?
- ◆ What is he asking for from his followers?
- ◆ After listening to this reading, how would you describe "the attitude of Christ"?

Third Reading of Gospel
- ◆ How does this speak to your life this week?
- ◆ Do you feel called to be different? In what ways?
- ◆ What is one quality you need to develop that will help you to have "an attitude of Christ"?

Closing Prayer
Bring together petitions and prayers of thanksgiving.

Gospel Readings
- Week 1: "Faith the Size of a Mustard Seed"; Luke 17:5-10 (before October 4, 1992)
- Week 2: "Cleansing of the Ten Lepers"; Luke 17:11-19 (before October 11, 1992)
- Week 3: "The Pabable of the Persistent Widow"; Luke 18:1-8 (before October 18, 1992)
- Week 4: "Parable of the Pharisee and the Tax Collector"; Luke 18:9-14 (before World Youth Day—October 25, 1992).

Modern-Day Heroes and "Sheroes"

As a special event or as part of a gathering ministry, introduce the theme for World Youth Day and present some background informa-

tion on it (see "Getting Started" in this manual). Since the theme focuses on living the faith and sharing the story of Christ, divide the youths in groups of three or four and assign them to select a modern hero or "shero," someone who lives the faith of Christ.

After they have chosen someone, they are to prepare a brief presentation, which can include music, posters, slides, videos, drama, or other creative forms. Allow one or two weeks for the groups to develop their presenta-

tions. Depending upon the number of youths involved, these presentations can be made together at one celebration in the week prior to World Youth Day, or they can be spread out as part of other programs in which the youths are involved, such as religious education sessions, youth-group meetings or a service group.

Yearbook of Youths

Develop a folder or "yearbook" of youths, which will be distributed to the parish or school community on World Youth Day (perhaps during a reception). In the folder, highlight youths from the parish or school who are involved in service, outreach, and leadership. Include such things as photos of and interviews with the youths, listings of their accomplishments, and so forth. This yearbook should be a youth-team project, with the young people taking the photographs, conducting the interviews, developing the art and graphics, and laying out the final copy. However, if an intergenerational approach is preferred, another option would be to feature within the yearbook, people of all ages who have shared the story!

A Heritage of Service and Advocacy

Sponsor a gathering of parish youths that will focus on the needs of the local community. This focus should be broad and should include direct service opportunities to persons and concerns that require advocacy from an organized group.

When the priority areas have been selected, divide the youths into teams to work with trained adults in developing projects and processes that will address these areas. These teams are responsible for organizing the effort and for developing service positions that can be filled by youths and adults in the parish or school. Contact all of the existing parish or school service and outreach groups and inform them of your undertaking.

The goal is to sponsor a "Living the Faith of Christ Service and Advocacy Fair." If parish-based, parishioners could attend the fair following the Sunday liturgies. If school-based, parents and members of the school community could attend during an "Open House" or a "Parents' Night."

At this fair, each service or advocacy opportunity would have a table display with posters and want ads describing the service opportunities. Service groups could enlist and interview candidates for the various activities at the fair or make follow-up appointments to provide further information. After groups have been formed, a special liturgy could be planned to commission these people in their mission and send them forth to share the story of Christ!

Discovering the Story of Our Parish (or School)

Invite a group of young people to research the history of their parish (school). They could work with an advisor to research any or all of the following:

- How was the church (school) established?
- How was the site selected and/or acquired?
- How was the name chosen?
- When was the church/school building erected?

This research could be done by examining church and diocesan records. Depending upon the age of the parish (school), the young people might be able to speak to parishioners (alumni) who can share a part of the history of the community. Once the information has been gathered, the youths could sponsor a "Birthday Party" for the entire community, where the story could be told and pictures, plans, and membership lists could be displayed. If there are any original parishioners or alumni they could be included in the presentation as special guests of honor.

Tom East
Archdiocese of Los Angeles

Celebrating World Youth Day with the Family

Encourage families to celebrate World Youth Day by honoring their young people and by becoming involved in all phases and activities of the celebration. Make it an annual tradition, similar to Mother's Day or Father's Day, but with the emphasis on praying, sharing the story, and affirming the youths, rather than on cards or gift giving. Invite extended family members to join together for this day and to share a special meal. Tell stories of the family and the heritage of faith as you gather around the table. The meal could conclude with a blessing of each youth.

A Family's Blessing for Youth

Dear God our Creator, who loves us as a parent,
we thank you for entrusting (insert name of
youth) to our family's special care.

Bless this precious son/daughter with faith,
courage, and enthusiasm as he/she goes forth as a
sign of Youth love in the world today.

---

*Blessing courtesy of Sr. Joan Vanderziden, SJC,
Port-Au-Prince, Trinidad*

Other family blessings can be found in the following resources:

The *Book of Blessings* (Collegeville, Minn.: The Liturgical Press):

- Order for the Blessing of a Family (nos. 40-61)
- Order for the Annual Blessing of Families in their Own Homes (nos. 68-89)
- Order for the Blessing of Baptized Children (nos. 139-155 and 170-173)
- Order for the Blessings of Sons and Daughters (nos. 174-194).

The *Catholic Household Blessings and Prayers* (Washington, D.C.: USCC Office for Publishing and Promotion Services):

- Blessings for a Family or Household (p. 206)
- Daily Blessing of a Child (p. 227)

The *Book of Family Prayers and Blessings* (Washington, D.C.: USCC Office for Publishing and Promotion Services).

A One-Day Retreat Model

Reflection for the Day: "God Has Something Prepared for Me"
(cf. 2 Tm 4:8)

The themes that will be developed during the day are presented here. The practical organizational elements remain at the discretion of those preparing the Retreat Day. A suggested timetable is given however.

RETREAT SESSION

9:00 a.m.   **Orientation (Choir or Recorded Songs)**

9:30 a.m.   **Opening Prayer Daniel 3:52-88 (Choral Recitation by Two Sides)**

10:00 a.m.   **First Theme: *"Color Your Dreams"***

Development of the Theme

◆ What is your living reality (e.g., cultural background; economic situation; relationship with your parents and other members of your family; environment in which you have grown up)?

◆ What are your dreams and uncertainties? What would you like to be in life? What are your plans for the future?

◆ What are your aptitudes and talents? What can you do and what do you like to do? What do you have an aptitude for (e.g., music, sports, literature)?

◆ The exposition of the theme, including the active participation of the youths, should not exceed one hour.

◆ In conclusion, the presenter can highlight the origin of all these uncertainties and questions expressed by the young people, and therefore highlight how to relate them to the Author of the talents they possess.

11:15 a.m.   **Break (Songs to Create Atmosphere)**

11:45 a.m.   **Second Theme: *"Why My Dreams Are Gloomy"***

Development of the Theme

◆ Various elements exist that condition the lives of youths and influence their behavior. Among them are the following: poverty, violence, injustice, discrimination, lack of understanding, envy, hatred, illnesses, physical and intellectual limitations, lack of cultural adjustment, emotional conflicts, and so forth.

◆ What are some occasions on which these negative aspects have predominated? All of these negative aspects prevent youths from developing or fulfilling themselves according to their wishes or dreams; all of these constitute obstacles for the realization of a plan in their lives. (This moment may be used to review the Ten Commandments. One could also construct a comparative chart of the values for different generations.)

◆ The theme should not last more than one hour and fifteen minutes, including the active participation of the youths.

1:00 p.m.   **Lunch and Games**

3:15 p.m.   **Third Theme: *"Start Dreaming Again"***

Penitential Rite and Confessions

Suggested Readings

– Parable of the Talents (Mt 25: 14-30)

– Parable of the Prodigal Son (Lk 15:11-32)

– Parable of the Pharisee and the Publican (Lk 18:9-14)

– Ephesians 4:17-30

– Psalm 50

- In the light of the Word the two former themes can be recalled so as to bring the youths to the idea that it is God who calls them to be someone in life in as much as they have been created in his image and likeness, and that in their hands has been placed the work of the same God (cf. Gen 1:26-27; Ps 8). Sin is, without doubt, the big obstacle that impedes them from fulfilling the plan of God in their lives.

- While the young people make their confessions, a climate of silence and prayer is recommended.

- Activities may be promoted such as reflecting or praying on the theme of pardon and of reconciliation.

4:30 p.m.   Break (Songs)

4:45 p.m.   Fourth Theme:
*"Sharing My
Dreams with Others"*

Development of the Theme

- The experience of sin has made young people see what they have lost (the Prodigal Son), but at the same time has recalled them to the right path: "I will rise up and return to the house of my father." One recalls the attitude of the publican, which earned him a pardon. . . . The gifts of the father (new clothes, new sandals, ring, a welcome celebration) signify what the young man means to his father. . . . The attitude of the father is an example for the adult. In its silence, it has much to say to youths and adults. There are adults in whom young people can confide and from whom they can learn.

- The road to recovery is not made by the youths alone; others—youths and adults—walk with them. Some have a longer road to walk or need help on the road. One thinks of the poor, the ignorant, the weak, those who suffer. The same Father waits for them also.

- What the young people have discovered today can be shared with other youths who are passing through similar situations. From today on the youths have a greater mission in life: to share their dreams—new dreams, dreams of life, dreams of the son who has found again the house of his father, dreams that began to be realized by the fact of having already covered part of the road. Perhaps, there exists someone with whom each young person desires to share his or her dreams; perhaps, there exist dreams that now are capable of being accomplished after the positive retreat experience.

It would be good to end the retreat with a celebration of the Eucharist. During the Offertory, an offering can be made of the "resolutions" or "promises" of the dreams the young people wish to realize.

**6:00 p.m.   Break (Preparation
for the Eucharist)**

**6:30 p.m.   Celebration of
the Eucharist**

- Renewal of the promises of baptism during the Creed

- Offering of the "dreams" that they hope to fulfill.

*Reverend Miguel A. Villegas
Covina, California*

Evangelization Training Session for Youths

Called to Spread the Message of Christ!

The following program provides a format for training youths to be evangelists, to help others to share the story of Christ! The words "evangelization" and "evangelist," often bring about fear and confusion to many people.

If you mention these words around young people, they often think of TV evangelists or Bible-toting preachers. Either way, these are not words that sit well with them. Young people need to know that they, too, are called to share the Good News of Christ with others. They also need to know that they do have the gifts and talents to share that news with others, and that they probably do so without even realizing it.

The purpose of this activity is to help young people realize that they are able to share the Good News of Christ with others. This will be done through a variety of exercises and discussions that will focus on invitation, welcome, relational ministry, and sharing the Good News.

This activity is designed to last about 4 1/2 hours, with a meal break included. If those in the group do not know each other, it would be good to have an icebreaker at the beginning of the session. Throughout the day, participants will be breaking into groups of two or three and groups of six or seven, therefore it would be beneficial to have people who can act as small-group facilitators.

Session Schedule

11:00 a.m.   Evangelization and Evangelists

- Large-group sharing question: What do these words mean to you?

11:05 a.m.   Large-Group Presentation and Sharing

- Picture Jesus as an evangelist as described by the group: How would he call his first apostles?

- Now picture him as we would hope him to be: How would he call his first apostles? (Optional: have a few of the youths act out the two different scenes.)

11:10 a.m.   Discussion

- What is the difference between the two styles?

11:15 a.m.   Brief Presentation: "Jesus Calls Us to Share the Good News—to Be an Evangelist"

- You do not need to be afraid of what it means to evangelize.

- You can and do evangelize others in many ways without realizing it.

- Today, you will see how easy and nonthreatening it can be to share the message of Jesus.

11:20 a.m.   Small-Group Discussion (Break into Groups of Two or Three)

- Why are you involved in youth ministry?

- Who invited you to become involved in youth ministry?

- What was it about them that attracted you to becoming involved?

11:30 a.m.   Large-Group Feedback

- Have everyone reassemble into the large group and share some of their responses to the small-group discussion questions. By now, they should be able to elaborate on the following:

- How can we invite others to join our community?

- How do we extend a welcome to other people?

- How do we include others and promote relationships?
- How do we share the Good News?

11:50 a.m. Presentation: "Invitation"

♦ How do we invite young people to participate in parish programs and activities?

♦ What is the most effective way to reach out? Is it through bulletin announcements or posters? How important is the personal touch?

11:55 a.m. Small-Group Discussion (Break into Groups of Six or Seven)

♦ Each group will need some newsprint and marking pens for use in their discussions.

♦ Share the ways in which your youth ministry currently reaches out to uninvolved people.

♦ You are the "Reach Out" team at your parish. Your team needs to develop and implement a plan in which you could better personalize your approach to reaching out and inviting young people to become involved in parish youth ministry programs. A few questions to ask: Who are these people? Where are they? How do we get in touch with what they need?

12:25 p.m. Large-Group Feedback

♦ Have each group share the plans that they just developed in the small-group discussions.

12:45 p.m. Lunch

1:30 p.m. Talk: "Welcoming"

♦ Youths often come to a youth ministry function, but they never come back because they feel lost and uninvited.

♦ Adult youth workers can reach out to people, but we need more than adults; youths need to be welcomed by other young people.

♦ How do we make young people feel welcome at a youth ministry gathering?

- *Greeting:* Are there people who greet others as they come in the door?

- *Introducing:* Do we introduce these people to others through large-group announcements or does a smaller group take them around and help them meet new people?

- *Invitation to Return:* Do we let these people know we want them around by telling them to come back to the next event?

- *Send Them Out Two by Two:* Knowing that young people like to do things in pairs and tend to have more courage that way, let's take advantage of it and set up our welcoming and inviting teams into teams of two.

1:45 p.m. "Welcoming Skills" (Break into Groups of Three)

♦ When instructing the young people to break into triads, if possible, have them join with others they do not know.

♦ Each youth takes a turn being the "new" person who is coming to youth ministry for the first time; the other two people will do the welcoming. Take five minutes for each person than switch. Give different settings for each welcoming, such as a social, a retreat, or a youth ministry gathering.

2:00 p.m.   Large-Group Feedback

◆ Have the youths rejoin the large group and discuss how they felt in the various small-group situations.

– When you were the "new" person, how did you feel?

– How did you feel when you were the greeter?

– Could you be a greeter?

– Any helpful insights? Comments?

2:15 p.m.   Small-Group Discussion (Break into Groups of Three)

◆ Discuss the topic: "Promoting Relationships: Letting Others Know That They Matter.

– How do you make friends?

– How did you and your closest friend(s) become so close?

– Is there a person in your youth ministry that you became close to, who you might not have become close to in another situation? Explain.

2:25 p.m.   Presentation: "Including Others and Promoting Relationships"

◆ Become interested in other people's interests and activities.

◆ You are not called to become everyone's best friend, but to be able to know and appreciate that person for being who he or she is.

◆ Being able to relate to other people is very important.

◆ Take the time to get to know other people.

2:35 p.m.   Stretch Break

2:45 p.m.   Presentation: "Before We Can Share the Good News, We Need to Be the Good News"

◆ Friendship in the Christian community: what makes us different? There is a realization that

– God loves us first, despite our faults and mistakes;

– God loves everyone;

– God loves always.

◆ Jesus the perfect example of love and compassion:

– Loves first (e.g., adulteress, Zachaeus);

– Loves everyone (e.g., children, apostles, tax collectors);

– Loves always (despite being crucified, he forgave those who killed him).

◆ Jesus calls us to do the same:

– Love first (no matter what the person is like);

– Love everyone (reach outside our circle of friends);

◆ Love always (even if that person does not become one of our close friends, God calls us to love and accept that person).

2:55 p.m.   Reflection Question: How Are You Called to Share the Good News?

◆ Christ is the Good News and, by our baptism, we are called to share that Good News with others. Through our inviting and welcoming, we can be the Good News to people.

◆ Recognizing people's stereotypes about evangelization, how can we share the Good News of Jesus with others?

3:00 p.m.   Small-Group Discussion (Break into Groups of Six or Seven)

◆ Knowing what you know about Jesus and his message, What do you think young people need to hear?

3:10 p.m.   Large-Group Feedback

◆ Have the young people rejoin the larger group and discuss their small-group reflections.

3:20 p.m.   Individual Reflection

◆ What is one message in which you really believe?

◆ How can you share that message with others?

3:25 p.m.   Evaluation and Summary

◆ Develop and distribute an Evaluation Form for the training day. After allowing time for completion of the evaluation, invite the youths to reflect on and share in a large-group setting the following question:

– How do you feel now about reaching out and welcoming young people? How do you feel about sharing and being the Good News?

3:30 p.m.   Conclusion

◆ Develop a prayer service to conclude the training day or use the one provided in this manual. Utilize the theme of "commissioning," focusing on Matthew 28:16-20.

Edward O'Connor
Office of Youth Ministry
Archdiocese of Los Angeles

An Adult Learning Session
Communicating with Teens

Goal

At the end of the session, the participants will have acquired tools to help them better communicate with teenagers. Effective communication is a two-way process: sharing your own values, stories, and morals and listening to and hearing what someone else is saying.

Objectives

1. The adults will remember vividly the feelings of teenage years and the needs that people at this stage of life require.

2. Participants will understand nonverbal communication and how it affects conversations with teenagers.

3. Participants will learn both listening and speaking skills that will make communicating with teens easier.

Overview

There are many elements of good communication, and it takes years of practice and effort to develop the skills necessary to be a good communicator. All the teens with whom I have worked want adults not only to teach them but also to "just listen" to them. They want adults to understand, to empathize, to respect their opinions, and "to hear what they are afraid to say." I questioned the young girl who made the last statement, and she said that adults really need to encourage her to speak sometimes because she is afraid to disagree on some issues. I also hear continually from teenagers that they wish their parents would remember what it was like to be their age.

Adults must not be afraid to "teach" values but in so doing, they must remember that it is important to listen and to phrase appropriately what we want to say to youths so our response does not close off dialogue and openness.

Keeping the comments of these teenagers in mind, and realizing that the majority of teenagers I see in my counseling practice feel unheard and misunderstood, I have divided this session into three parts: (1) a journey into the past that helps the adult participants to remember themselves as teenagers; (2) communication skills, both listening to and speaking with; and (3) nonverbal communication. These parts can be used separately or in any combination, according to the needs of your group.

I. Understanding Your Teenager— A Trip into the Past

♦ The following are needed:

– newsprint on which the discussion questions for each section below have been written; and

– a relaxed, comfortable environment where small-group sharing is possible.

Process

♦ Have participants gather into groups of four to six people.

♦ Ask that they get comfortable and relaxed and open their minds to follow as you lead them on a journey into the past.

The Journey: Give these or similar instructions to the group:

The Present: To begin, I would like each of you to get to know the people in your group by discussing the following topics:

- ◆ Introduce yourself to the group. Include a description of your family in the introduction.

- ◆ What cause is important to you?

- ◆ Who is God? Tell something about your faith.

Age Twenty-Three: We are going back in time now. This will be easier for some of you than for others. Try to visualize yourself at the age of twenty-three. You might be finishing your education, beginning your family, starting a new career, or living a carefree single life. Is it a happy time? A lonely time? Where are you living? What do you look like? When you as a group are ready, please discuss the following:

- ◆ Who are your best friends? Why have you chosen them?

- ◆ How do you spend your time?

- ◆ What is most important to you?

- ◆ Where does God fit into your life?

High School Graduation (Approximately Age Eighteen): We are going further back now. Please think about the day you graduated from high school. Where is the graduation? How big is the class? What color are the robes? Who has come there just to see you? As a group, please share the following:

- ◆ What do you like?

- ◆ Who is your best friend? Your favorite musician? Your favorite movie?

- ◆ What questions do you have about God? The Church?

- ◆ What is your greatest need?

Age Thirteen: High School is just beginning, and you have to enter that big building. How do you feel? You are just starting to develop sexually, your body is different. Are you comfortable with it? Some days, you feel all grown up; some days you are still a child. How tall are you? Who are your

friends? What plans do you have? What are your dreams? When you are ready, please share the following:

- ◆ Tell something good about yourself.

- ◆ What is the most important thing in the world to you?

- ◆ How do you feel about your parents? What do you want from them?

- ◆ What is your greatest need right now?

[Note: The above regression process will take different lengths of time for different groups. The questions and statements used should also be adapted to each specific group so that the leader can judge when it is time to move on from one stage to another.]

Remaining at Age Thirteen: Please attempt to stay at age thirteen and see how you would deal with our world today, in which the following statistics prevail:

- ◆ Over 70 percent of 12th graders are regular alcohol users.

- ◆ The average age of first sexual intercourse is fifteen.

- ◆ There are 200 million street children in the world.

- ◆ One in four girls and one in ten boys is sexually abused.

- ◆ The average twelve- to fifteen-year-old spends $35.20 per week on himself or herself.

- ◆ In the United States, there are more cars per family than children.

- – Do you have concerns you would like to discuss?

- – Can you go to your parents or to other adults?

- – What would make it easier for you to talk with them?

The Present: Please magically return to adulthood. Discuss the following questions:

- ◆ How can you use this exercise to communicate better with your teenagers?

- ◆ Take one issue (e.g., sexuality, materialism, substance abuse) and discuss how you as thirteen-year-olds would see it versus how you would see it as adults. How can these two viewpoints be shared with respect for one another?

II. Communication Skills

- ◆ The following are needed:
- – comfortable seats
- – tape recorder

Process

- ◆ Participants will practice assertive communication and active listening in the following exercises.

Assertive Communication is appropriate, direct, honest, and contains respectful confrontation. "I" statements are one popular type of assertive communication, and in this section we will practice formulating them.

"I" Statements: An "I" statement is defined by three parts:

- ◆ A nonjudgmental and objective description of another's behavior.
- ◆ A description of the concrete effects it has on you.
- ◆ An expression of how it makes you feel.

Example: When you talk back to me (part 1), I get really angry and upset (part 2), because I don't feel you respect me (part 3).

Exercise: Have the participants practice "I" statements for typical problems encountered in their lives (particularly those dealing with teenagers), for example:

- – a messy room;
- – loud music;
- – coming home late;
- – dressing all in black;
- – hating church;
- – not wanting to be seen with their parents; and
- – being involved sexually.

"You" Statements: These statements are obviously the opposite of the "I" statements in the above exercise. Beware! They turn people away—especially teenagers. For example:

- ◆ You dummy, don't you have better sense?
- ◆ You make me furious!
- ◆ Why don't you grow up!
- ◆ You blew it again; you just can't be trusted!

Active Listening. An active listener is an effective listener. An active listener is respectful and nonjudgmental. He or she asks clarifying questions. He or she listens to nonverbal as well as verbal messages.

Exercise: Ask the participants to consider the above definition and prepare to become active listeners. Then present the following list of statements about listening made by teenagers. You can read the list, or if you have the time and resources, you can have the teenagers make an audiotape of these statements along with any others they might wish to add.

- ◆ It really makes me mad when I say something and my parents just smile and say, "Yes dear."
- ◆ My parents only half listen while they keep doing whatever they were doing.
- ◆ My dad always says something like, "It's not as bad as you think" or "You'll get over it."
- ◆ My opinions aren't respected.
- ◆ I want to be treated just like my parents treat their friends. They stop what they're doing and are polite and listen.
- ◆ I want to get the whole story out before they give their opinion.
- ◆ I want them to respect my feelings and not make me feel stupid.
- ◆ I don't like sarcastic comments and put-downs.
- ◆ I'm expected to listen to them and not interrupt, and I want the same treatment.

- ◆ We talk best at dinner, away from the TV, where everyone is really listening.

Exercise: Discuss the following questions:

- ◆ What obstacles do you see in your situation that cause difficulty in talking with and listening to teenagers?
- ◆ Effective communication of values and morals requires that we not only talk but listen to what children are saying. Many times, we need to hear the message/meaning behind the words. What method can you develop to make active listening a part of your communication with teenagers?

III. Nonverbal Communication

- ◆ No special supplies are needed for this part of the session.

Process

- ◆ Through the following exercises, participants will learn how better to deal with noncommunicative teenagers.

Nonverbal Communication: Teenagers are renowned experts on nonverbal communication. Many parents refer to it as "that look." We as adults must learn to understand this form of communication so that we can enable teenagers to bypass this behavior and verbalize their feelings. The trick is to empathize with their feelings and to let them know how you feel.

Exercise: Ask someone from the group to be your parent as you role play some nonverbal behavior:

- ◆ You are a 10th grade girl, arriving home from school. You walk in, throw your books down, go to the kitchen, slam the refrigerator door, look at your parent, and in answer to "How was your day?" you answer, "Fine." (The hidden fact here is that the person you really wanted to go to Homecoming with just asked your best friend.)

Exercise: Discuss methods of dealing with nonverbal behaviors:

- Ask if you can help.
- If help is refused, back off and wait for another opportunity.
- Respect the teenager's right to privacy and to feel as he or she does.
- Let the teenager know that you had similar feelings as a teenager; that you are human too.
- When the teenager is finally able to express his or her feelings, DON'T say something along the lines of "You should not feel that way." When a person feels his or her feelings are being judged, he or she will immediately stop talking.
- Use "I" statements.
- After the teenager has finished talking, ask yourself if you have done all that is needed. Sometimes, just talking makes the pain go away.

Exercise: Have the group role play scenes pertaining to nonverbal messages. This can be done in small groups or as a large group, depending on the type of participants and the group size. Ask the participants to use their personal experiences. You should have a few examples, such as the following, to get them started:

- Your teenager will not eat (someone jokingly said she was fat).
- Your son is pacing the floor, swearing nothing is wrong (you know he just talked to his girlfriend).
- Your sensitive, caring son suddenly turns macho (someone called him gay).

Exercise: End the session with a reminder that "poor communication" is named the number-one problem in relationships of all kinds. Remind them of the following:

- Think positively.
- Remember their youth.
- Speak in "I" statements.
- Listen with respect and attention.
- Always be aware of what teenagers *aren't* saying.
- Don't quit—it's a slow process to perfection!

Sharon Hoffman
Gaithersburg, Maryland

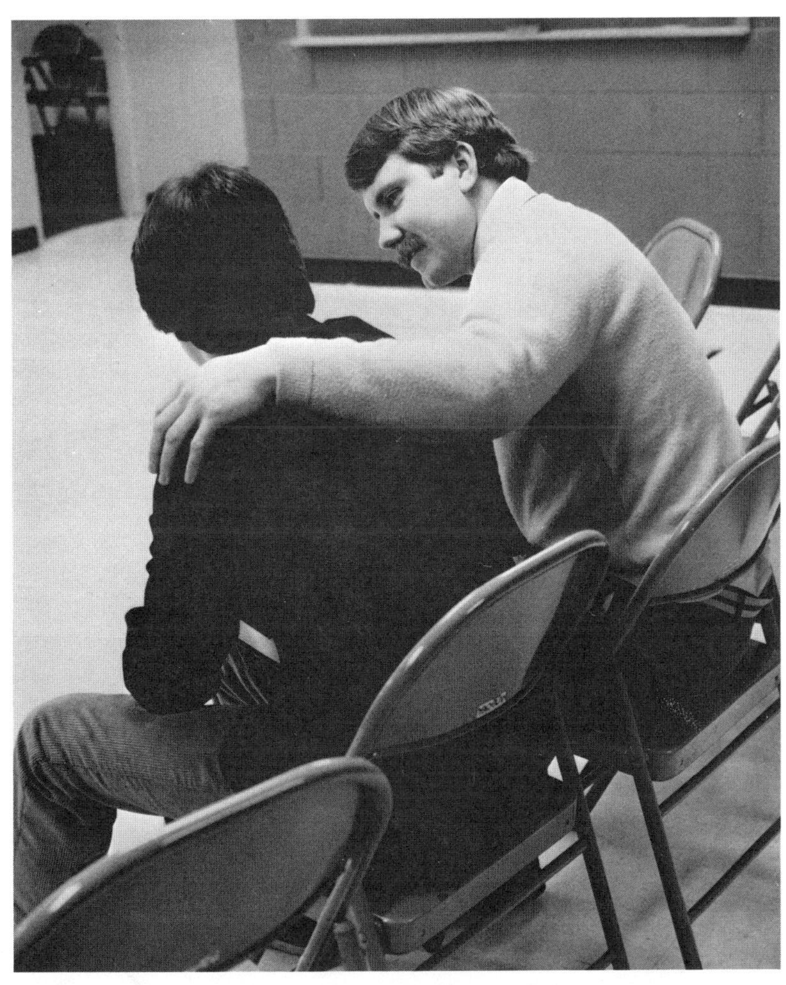

Suggestions for Prayer and Worship

PREPARATION

Considering All Options

Preparing prayer and worship opportunities for the whole parish or school is part of a total plan for celebrating World Youth Day. Parish weekend liturgies or an all-school Mass are the most obvious ways to focus attention on youth, but consider these other options as well:

- A special prayer service on the evening of religious education sessions that parents are invited to attend. Plans might also include a pot-luck supper and/or recognition of youth who have been involved in service or leadership events.

- A Sunday evening prayer service. This could take place in the late afternoon or early evening, followed by a social event, speaker, or presentation.

- A written prayer service or family prayer (see "Parish and School Activities"), nicely printed and designed, to be used at all parish meetings during the month of October. A similar prayer opportunity could be designed for student council and club meetings or to be prayed in all classes the week of World Youth Day.

Gathering the Right People

The hardest part of implementing any plan involving parish worship is usually getting the right people together. As advocates for youth, our main task is to communicate with pastors, liturgists, music ministers, and others who have responsibility for the whole community. My advice is to invite rather than avoid persons you have experienced as uncooperative in the past.

Youths are a gift to our communities from God. Let the value of that gift be your invitation to them to contribute their expertise to a special planning committee on World Youth Day. Let each person do his or her job. Your goal is to see that youths and parents are also involved in the process.

Being Realistic

Strive for a plan that has a good chance for success. Remember, you are trying to improve attitudes toward young people. A good plan will highlight the talents and contributions of youths and still be in harmony with the parish style of worship.

Keeping the Theme in Context

The theme of every Mass is the Paschal Mystery. From week to week, we focus on particular ideas, scripture passages, and awarenesses, but the basic reason for gathering to pray always remains the same: we come together to remember actively Christ's dying and rising. That is the heritage (the story) we want to rediscover continually. That is the story we want to share.

Considering Current Events

What are the local and world events that are currently shaping the lives of your community? What impact are the national elections, the annual harvest, local school events such as homecoming week, and other situations having upon the community's consciousness of youths? Worship celebrations on World Youth Day should help to shape those attitudes. You may need to pay particular attention to the various viewpoints surrounding Columbus Day. My suggestion is to focus on the encounter of cultures, which continues today in most communities. Insights might be gained from how adults encounter youth culture and vice versa. How youths celebrate the unique cultural heritages among their peers is another possibility for prayer and reflection.

Evaluating

Take time to evaluate any worship plans that were implemented so that successes can be acknowledged and difficulties can be addressed next year or in the coming months. Evaluation becomes the first step of planning for World Youth Day 1993.

PLANNING A WEEKEND LITURGY

The cornerstone of worship plans to celebrate the World Youth Day theme, "Live the Faith, Share the Story!" will likely be preparation for the weekend parish liturgies. Because of this additional focus, consider this weekend as the time to announce and implement an apprenticeship program for youths in the liturgical ministries.

Several adults involved in preparing the church environment, or as greeters, readers, eucharistic ministers, song leaders, or accompanists, will train youth apprentices and be their mentors as they take on these ministries in the coming months. These adults and youths are then acknowledged at the weekend Masses.

Other suggestions are divided into the four movements of liturgy: (1) gather; (2) listen; (3) respond; and (4) send forth (commission).

Gathering

Spend extra time preparing a sense of hospitality and welcome on World Youth Day. Make an effort to invite young people who are not regular participants.

- Have youths at the entrances to church pass out "holy cards" that they have made, featuring quotes from or brief stories about the lives of youthful saints. These quotes might make good banner ideas, too.

- Find pictures or icons of saints from other cultures or of Christ, and place them in various locations around the church (e.g., in the entrance ways).

- Have children dress in the attire of their cultural heritage. They can be part of an entrance procession and carry flowers that are placed near the altar and ambo.

- Emphasize the idea of homecoming (see "Homily Suggestions") by having "Class of (Year)" name badges at all the entrances or have youths create name badges with their school names. All students are invited to participate. Invite former and current school personnel to be present and recognized for their contributions over the years.

- Sing additional songs as people are gathering. Focus on diversity, unity, and discovery.

- **Suggested Hymns:** nos. 1, 2, 5, 6, 9, 10, 13, 24 (see section on "Music Suggestions," p. 25, for hymnals and corresponding titles).

Listening

The Liturgy of the Word is an opportunity to feature youths proclaiming the Scriptures, perhaps using multiple readers, particularly for the dialogue lines of the gospel. It is essential that they be well-prepared.

- Consider developing the homily suggestions made above.

- If young people have dressed in cultural attire have them each read petitions or stand next to the lector as the petitions are being read. If a parish or school has young people who speak different languages have them read their petitions in their native language and then read them in English.

- Have teens read selected "Belief Statements" from those developed at the National Youth Congress in November 1991. These statements could proceed the assembly's recitation of the Creed. Copies of the "Belief Statements" are available from your diocesan Office for Youth Ministry; the NCCB Secretariat for Family, Laity, Women and Youth (202-541-3040); or the National Federation for Catholic Youth Ministry (202-636-3825).

- **Suggested Hymns:** nos. 3, 11, 20, 21, 22, 23 (see section on "Music Suggestions," p. 25, for hymnals and corresponding titles).

Responding

The Liturgy of the Eucharist might begin with a more deliberate Preparation Rite, during which youths carry forward the cloth, candles, *Sacramentary,* bread, and wine and set the table.

- Consider having the musicians play something "youthful" in the background as the ritual action occurs.

- Consider using one of the Eucharistic Prayers approved for Masses with Children, particularly II or III.

- If your parish is bilingual consider using a bilingual set of acclamations as an act of solidarity with Christians in other parts of the world.

- **Suggested Hymns:** nos. 7, 8, 16, 17, 25, 27 (see section on "Music Suggestions," p. 25, for hym-

nals and corresponding titles).

Sending Forth

The concluding rites should help focus on our mission to live as believers in Christ and should flow from the previous liturgical actions. During the meditation after communion consider having a brief slide presentation, featuring youths involved in various service experiences; this might be set to Rod Stewart's recording of "Forever Young" (Warner), De-Garmo and Key's "Hand in Hand" (Forefront), or another appropriate contemporary song.

- Invoke a blessing over the youths, similar to the custom on Mother's Day or Father's Day. Ask the assembly to be seated and then have all children and youths stand. Use the "Solemn Blessing" from the *Sacramentary,* nos. 13, 14, 15.

- **Suggested Hymns:** nos. 4, 12, 14, 15, 18, 19, 26 (see section on "Music Suggestions," p. 25, for hymnals and corresponding titles).

SCRIPTURE REFLECTIONS

Thirtieth Sunday in Ordinary Time

One approach would be to remember Homecoming Week or some other special anniversary celebration that was celebrated in your high school. (That may be easier for some of us than others!) Homecoming Week usually involves special activities, celebrations, a pep rally, a football game, and a dance.

Even the faculty and administration get involved in the skits and activities. What do these efforts hope to achieve? Part of their purpose is to cheer on the football team in the big game, but we realize that part of the intent is to build a sense of spirit and tradition in the school community. (It is easier to focus on this intent when the team loses!) Developing attitudes of cooperation and community based on a sense of belonging is the key to understanding Homecoming.

The Scriptures for the weekend during which we celebrate World Youth Day challenge us to develop Christ-like attitudes of humility, perseverance, and solidarity with the poor and oppressed in this world. We might call them *"BE-attitudes."*

Sirach 35:12-14,16-18

The author calls us to recognize our God as "One who knows no favorites" and "who hears the cry of the oppressed." We might ask who are the least-favored persons in our own schools, workplaces, neighborhoods, and world community? Who are the people who get left out of Homecoming celebrations? What labels do we use to identify these people? What stereotypes are we guilty of perpetuating? What actions are we taking to align ourselves with these persons, to aid them in becoming a part of the full community? What is one specific effort we can make individually or in cooperation with others to demonstrate a change in our attitude?

2 Timothy 4:6-8,16-18

Paul's letter to Timothy was written at a time when the early Christian community that Timothy led was experiencing some of the day-to-day difficulties in trying to live with a common purpose. There were questions of leadership, authority, and direction. For Timothy, these questions began to undermine his desire to keep going in the midst of it all. Paul exhorts Timothy to "finish the race," "to keep the faith," and to "persevere" because the goal of helping to bring about the reign of God is worth his effort.

During Homecoming Week, the boy and girl chosen as Homecoming king and queen often are the most popular students—but not always. What change in attitude does it take for us to place confidence in unpopular leaders because we believe their values are more in line with ours?

Who are the current leaders in whom we place our trust? Who are our heroes, the persons we admire? Do they exhibit the qualities of perseverance, dedication, and sense of purpose that Paul suggests are worthy of our admiration? Do we strive for these same qualities in our own roles as leaders within our peer group, family, church community, or workplace?

Luke 18:9-14

This passage from Luke recounts a parable Jesus told about the Pharisee and the tax collector who are in the temple praying. Which one has the attitude that Jesus says is necessary? By all outward expectations, the Pharisee has done what is required. He has fasted twice a week and given his tithe. But his attitude is contempt for those who, like the tax collector, do not appear to measure up to the same standard.

The tax collector's prayer acknowledges complete dependence on God's mercy. His attitude demonstrates an openness to God's grace. We might assume from the parable that he still needs to improve in doing good works, but Jesus suggests that the tax collector's attitude is right and will eventually bring him justification.

On this World Youth Day, let

us consider what it would be like if the whole world adopted the attitudes of *idealism* and *enthusiasm,* which are a gift of adolescence. Could we let go of our previous assumptions about the prospects for world peace? Could we look past the language and cultural differences that mark the roots of racism? Could we grow in a self-respect grounded in God's love for each of us that would confront the addictions of drugs, consumerism, and sexual abuse? It is especially disturbing to know that youth-to-youth violence, incidents of racism, and various addictions are increasing in the emerging generation. It makes the need for youth ministry even more important.

The story of Christ is our heritage and our story. Maybe we need a Homecoming Weekend in our parishes and Catholic schools to focus on that spirit, on our tradition of ministry and service, and on our common mission and purpose. We may lose a few football games along the way, but we know that what is most important is to develop Christ-like attitudes that will help to bring about the heavenly reign of God.

HOMILY SUGGESTIONS

To add some contemporary focus to a prepared homily, consider beginning the time with a brief story developed by teens and recounted for the assembly.

Settings

The setting for the story might be a conversation in the high school cafeteria, at the Homecoming dance, on the sidelines during the Homecoming game, at the student council meeting after the announcement of Homecoming elections, or in the local fast-food restaurant during Homecoming Week, just to give a few examples.

Storyline

The focus of the story might be drawn from any of the scripture readings for that Sunday: the God "who knows no favorites" from Sirach; Paul's encouragement to Timothy to "keep the faith"; or the Pharisee's prayer, thanking God he is not like the lowly tax collector. It might be a conversation between a popular and an unpopular girl in the cafeteria; between the Homecoming king or queen and a "wallflower" at the dance; between a coach and a player at the game; a debate on true leadership at the student council meeting; or a confrontation between rival cliques at the restaurant.

Variables

Consider how issues of race, culture, and economic status change the dynamics of the story. Are there changes when the perspective is the younger or the older generation? Would it be different at a Catholic school? There are many options. The story could be recounted by two teens.

Other Concerns

The presiding priest needs to be part of the creative process so that he can preach effectively. If two youths recount the story make sure they are confident of their roles.

MUSIC SUGGESTIONS

The following hymns are offered as suggestions only. Use creativity and resourcefulness to plan and design a liturgy that reflects your own community and young people. The numbers referenced in the above section on "Planning a Weekend Liturgy" are shown here preceding the hymn's title. Those that follow each title indicate numerical placement within a specific hymnal.

Glory and Praise Hymnal

1. "Anthem," no. 83
2. "I Rejoiced," no. 106

3. "The Cry of the Poor," no. 93
4. "All My Days," no. 2

New People's Mass Book Hymnal

5. "For All the Saints," no. 187
6. "In Christ There Is No East or West," no. 103
7. "Where Charity and Love Prevail," no. 659
8. "Let Us Break Bread Together," no. 661

Lead Me, Guide Me Hymnal

9. "Come By Here," no. 218
10. "We've Come This Far by Faith," no. 225
11. "Lead Me, Guide Me," no. 168
12. "This Little Light of Mine," no. 190

Worship III Hymnal

13. "O Christ the Great Foundation," no. 618
14. "The Church of Christ in Every Age," no. 626

Gather Hymnal

15. "Bring Forth the Kingdom," no. 280
16. "I Will Not Die," no. 281
17. "We Have Been Told," no. 296
18. "The Harvest of Justice," no. 300
19. "We Are Called," no. 301
20. "Taste and See," no. 338

Celebration Series

21. "Taste and See," by Marty Haugen
22. "Come My Children," by David Haas

Music Issue and Other Hymnals

23. "Taste and See," by Bob Hurd
24. *"Envia Tu Espiritu,"* by Bob Hurd
25. *"Pan de Vida,"* by Bob Hurd
26. "Everlasting Your Love," by Bob Hurd
27. *"Misa De Las Americas,"* by Bob Hurd

A PRAYER SERVICE FOR WORLD YOUTH DAY 1992

Leader:

Let us begin with a moment of silence.   [*Pause.*]

Now, keeping that silent prayer, we make the gesture that signs us as all as Christians.

[*All make the sign of the cross, slowly, deliberately.*]

Leader:

All of us have used a camera at some time or other to take a snapshot of friends, family, a special place, a special occasion, a humorous moment, something we want to remember. But our memories are filled with snapshots taken with our mind's eye. I invite you to take the next couple of minutes to recall one of those snapshots of a parent, a grandparent, a teacher, a friend, an older brother or sister, or another person who helped you discover something about what it means to be a believer in Christ.

[*During the reflection time consider playing the song "The Living Years," by Mike and the Mechanics/Atlantic Records, or a contemporary song that addresses issues of the generations. Depending on the size of the group, invite each person to share his or her snapshot with one or two others, or with the whole group. Conclude the sharing with the following prayer.*]

All:

Generous God,
we thank you for the gift of
   those persons
who have walked before us in
   faith.

They have helped us to know
   your goodness
and directed us toward your
   truth.

Our reflections on these special
   persons
remind us of our own responsibility
   to pass on the faith to others,
especially to the generations to
   come.

Through your grace,
may our lives give witness to
   your loving presence
and the spirit of Christ, in whose
   name we make this prayer.

Amen.

SONG

"For the Beauty of the Earth"
(Use verses one and three from the version published by Oregon Catholic Press.)

"For All the Saints"
(Chicago: J.S. Paluch Company, *New People's Mass Book,* no. 187.)

"The Living Years"
(Play the closing chorus.)

[*Or select an appropriate contemporary song.*]

READING

1 Corinthians 1:3-9

SILENT PRAYER

LITANY OF THANKS

Lord, our children and youths
are a blessing from you:

Response:
We thank you, Lord.

For their enthusiasm for life . . .
R/.

For their innocence and curiosity . . .
R/.

For their willingness to learn new things . . .
R/.

For their restlessness with words . . .
R/.

For their questions of authority . . .
R/.

For their emerging leadership . . .
R/.

For their creativity and imagination . . .
R/.

For their caring friendships . . .
R/.

For their willingness to serve others . . .
R/.

[*Other petitions may be added spontaneously.*]

Leader:

I invite you now to take a moment to think about a young person who may need an encouraging word, a sympathetic embrace, a sincere compliment, a thank-you, a listening ear, or just an extra measure of your time. Make a promise to yourself to follow up on your intention, and as you do so, say the first name of the person out loud. [*Names are spoken at random.*]

Leader:

Gathering our litany of thanks, we pray now in the words that Jesus taught us: [*All pray the Lord's Prayer:* Our Father . . .]

Leader:

Loving God,
from age to age you have given
  your Church
witnesses of your faithfulness
  and love.

On this World Youth Day,
we pray that our youth may
  become "new apostles" to
  the generations to come,
and faithful witnesses of your
  presence among us.

May each of us catch the spirit
  of discipleship
and grow in Christ-like attitudes
  of service, humility, and perseverance.

We ask this through Christ,
  our Lord.

Amen.

SONG

"This Little Light"

(Chicago: GIA Publications, *Lead Me, Guide Me Hymnal,* no. 190.)

[*Or select another appropriate contemporary song.*]

Alternate Prayer Text

Let us pray.

Loving God,
through the ages you have given
  your Church witnesses of
  your faithfulness and love.

On this World Youth Day,
we pray that our young people
  may become "new apostles"
  to the next generations,
and faithful witnesses of your
  presence among us.

May each of us live the faith
  and share the story,
growing in Christ-like attitudes
  of service, humility, and
  perseverance.

We ask this through Christ,
  our Lord.

Amen.

A World Youth Day Blessing

Lord, our children and youth
  are a blessing from you.

On this World Youth Day,
we ask that you bless them in
  a special way.

When they are discouraged and
  disappointed,
bless them with an enthusiasm
  for life.

Bless them with friends who are
  trustworthy and sincere,
who help them discover the joys
  of your creation and remain
  strong when faced with the
  negative pressures of life.

Bless their experiences in school
so that the knowledge they gain
  may help them face their futures with hope.

Bless their questions of authority
  and tradition.

May their directness challenge
  us all to work for justice and
  world peace.

Bless their families and loved
  ones
so that they may always know
  the height and depth, length
  and breadth of your love.

We ask this through Christ,
  our Lord.

Amen.

Thomas Tomaszek
Office of Youth Ministry
Diocese of Milwaukee

Stories of Young People

A TEXAN ADVENTURE

The young missionaries from the Diocese of Austin had no idea that a mere 500-mile journey would take them so far, challenge them so much, or bring them so much closer to God. But that is exactly what happened last July, when twenty-five American teenagers immersed themselves in Mexican culture and learned from devout Catholics on the other side of the border.

What they learned continues to astonish them: a whole new way of viewing their own life-styles, their relationships with God, and their ties to the Church.

As we all had hoped, the journey opened their eyes and their hearts, and many of them were called to action. Each day, the group visited yet another *rancho* or settlement. And each day, they came together to share what happened. Their reflections showed how God had moved these young people. They were stirred by the majestic sunsets and the awe-inspiring sunrises. Many of them saw God in the faces of the young and the old of the *ranchos* who were called to church by the clamoring of a bell. Many of them saw God in the crippled man, whose uncompromising faith was revealed in his kindness, humor, and humility. They saw God in the tears that were shed between two groups of people, who knew they would never see each other again.

In the span of one week, a group of young missionaries renewed their lives—and their faith, as well. In their own words, three of them tell how such a 500-mile journey made a difference in their lives.

✛ ✛ ✛ ✛ ✛ ✛ ✛ ✛

"I enjoyed watching the children's faces light up as they caught a ball. I just knew these kids were special. At all the missions, I loved working with the children because I knew that if I could share just one smile with every kid I met, I was doing work for the Lord. All the kids I met in Mexico are still in my prayers and in my heart" (*Duane Rodriguez, 15*).

✛ ✛ ✛ ✛ ✛ ✛ ✛ ✛

"Hot showers, soft beds, and make-up are only a few things I left behind on my experience to Arteaga. For one week, civilization as I knew it changed. The things I took for granted in the United States were simply a memory. The people who welcomed

As we had all hoped, the journey opened their eyes and their hearts, and many of them were called to action.

us, did so with open arms even though they knew nothing about us or our reasons for being there. The experience is not one that is forgotten or one that has ended. We have raised money to bring our friends from Arteaga and the surrounding missions to visit us. My life greatly changed upon my return home. I knew that my material things could never amount to their faith and love, and I hope that I can learn from their example" (*Stephanie Lara, 16*).

"All persons, at least once in their lives, have an experience that opens their eyes to the full power, glory, and compassion of God. For each individual, it is different. Some realize the power of God in the fury of a storm. Some see God's glory in a breathtaking sunrise. Yet others are taught the Lord's compassion through silent, humble works of others. I have been blessed with all three experiences through the grace of God, with the climax occurring on a mission trip to Arteaga.

"Our goal was to immerse ourselves in their culture and teach them about ours. In so doing, we found a common bond: our faith. The trip proved to me how catholic our Church and faith really are. Never in my life have I been witness to such deep faith. I had expected to see faces that had endured lives of quiet desperation, but instead I saw their eyes twinkle, their faces shine, and all because of their faith in God.

"The people of Arteaga and the surrounding communities all live at subsistence levels, but this doesn't bother them because they really don't care about material things, but rather about love, devotion, and compassion.

"When we talked among ourselves, we expressed how lucky we are in comparison to the people of Arteaga, because of our homes, cars, and other material accumulations. But actually, I believe the people of Arteaga are the lucky ones. They are people with extraordinary faith. They are the ones who live without the pressures of materialism. And I find myself questioning my own lifestyle. I find myself asking questions such as: Why do I need this? Why do I put importance on things other than a life of love committed to Jesus Christ?" (*Matt Kostelecky, 17*).

Love was the language of their week in Mexico. Some discovered their heritage, and all joined together as they lived their faith in the spirit of Jesus who calls us to love, reach out, and open our hearts to each other in faith.

Sr. Norma Gutierrez
Office of Youth Ministry
Diocese of Austin

A HIGH SIERRA MISSION

As a Catholic youth in today's world, I sometimes find it difficult to live as I feel God wants me to. Our society creates new obstacles for everyone each day, obstacles that without proper guidance could cause further problems.

Even though youths are sometimes thought to be irresponsible or incapable of making correct decisions, I have found that being involved with my parish Youth Ministry has allowed me to grow in many ways.

One form of growth is becoming closer to God. I do this by helping his people. When I say helping "his people" I am referring to the less fortunate of my community, those who are homeless. The fourth Sunday of every month I join my youth group and help out at our local soup kitchen downtown, called Loaves and Fishes. My youth group joins with another group and is in charge of preparing the meal for the day. This is a very large job because we are cooking a meal that feeds 600 people—God's people.

I receive a lot of inner gratification by helping the homeless. By giving just a few hours of my time and a little energy, I am part of helping to feed these many needy people. I feel as though it is something that God wants me to do. It brings me closer to him and, at the same time, I'm helping my community.

Our youths today all have it in them to be the wonderful people that God wants us to be, but not all of them have found a way to reach that goal with God. I feel fortunate that I have become involved with my church and community, because by doing so I have opened the door to a brighter future with God.

Dayle Navarro
Sacramento, California

Youths as Evangelizers

"Circumstances invite us to make special mention of the young. Their increasing number and growing presence in society and likewise the problems assailing them should awaken in everyone the desire to offer them with zeal and intelligence the Gospel ideal as something to be known and lived. And on the other hand, young people who are well trained in faith and prayer must become more and more the apostles of youth.

The Church counts greatly on their contribution . . ." (Paul VI, *On Evangelization in the Modern World* [*Evangelii Nuntiandi*], 72).

Paul VI, in his apostolic exhortation, calls attention to two important considerations for those of us who work with youths. First, youths need to be evangelized. None of us will argue with that. We are all well aware of the many challenges facing our young people today. The voices of materialism, secularism, sexual promiscuity, drugs, and alcohol clamor for their attention and allegiance. The breakdown of many families and the loss of cultural supports for living a Christian life have left many young people with little or no faith experience or religious instruction.

Yes! It responds in our heart, youths need to be evangelized. Let's do it! But Paul VI also shares something equally important when we consider youth evangelization. The youths themselves must be the evangelizers. Youth sharing the gospel with youth. That is not to say that adults do not have an important part to play. Parents are the first and primary teachers of their children in matters of faith. Priests, men and women religious, and youth ministers all have a vital part to play in the work of youth evangelization. Indeed, the whole parish community is called to live a life of holiness and service that will attract and support young people in living a Catholic Christian life.

Why do youths have an important part to play in the Church's task of evangelizing young people? Let me share with you what I see as the strengths of youths as evangelizers and what they need from us (adults) to succeed. There are four reasons why I think youths make great evangelizers:

---

1. Youths are zealous and idealistic.

Young people still dream. They still believe the world can be better. They want to make a difference. As a young person encounters Christ and experiences his personal love, the excitement of newfound faith coupled with youthful zeal produces a dynamism that is very attractive to other youths.

---

2. Youths speak the language.

Youths listen to other youths. Whether we like it or not, our young people look to and listen to their peers more than their parents. In their transition to adulthood, they are beginning to look less to Mom and Dad and more to their friends in answering some of life's questions. The opinions of their peers carry weight. I have seen a number of situations where one or two faith-filled teenagers have brought a large number of their friends back to Christ and life in the Church.

---

3. Youths keep the message simple.

All too often, we older folks make following the Lord too complex. We provide all sorts of religious instruction but neglect the simple message that Christ loves you and wants to be in a relationship with you. Don't get me wrong. Catechism is important, but the Christian life seems oppressive without experiencing the love and personal interest of the Lord. Youths do not provide theology. They share, "this is what Christ has done for me and he wants to be with you." Simple.

---

4. Youths have a tradition of speading the Good News.

The Bible and our tradition are full of illustrations of God using young people to spread his word and his work. The call of Jeremiah, "Say not, 'I am too young.' To whomever I send you, you shall go; whatever I command you, you shall speak" (Jer 1:7); and the call of Timothy, "Let no one have contempt for your youth, but set an example for those who believe, in speech, conduct, love, faith, and purity" (1 Tm 4:12) are well known to us. In addition, saints such as Maria Goretti, Theresa of Lisieux, Francis of Assisi, Louis-King of France, Francis Xavier, Bernadette, and Julia Billiart are examples of women and men who gave their lives to God at a young age and were used by God to advance the kingdom.

What must we do to assist our young people in their call to evangelism?

---

1. Young people need to be provided with opportunities to share their faith.

Often, we overlook the valuable resource that our young people can be in our evangelization efforts. All too often we lose our most enthusiastic young people to nondenominational groups and movements that offer them numerous ways to make significant contributions in the work of spreading the gospel. Forming youth retreat teams, music and drama troupes, student-led youth groups, mission trips to serve in poor areas, school bible studies and prayer meetings are a few examples of ways that young people can make a significant impact.

---

2. Young people need practical instruction in how to live the Christian life.

For any of us—young or old—to be effective evangelizers, we must be growing in our own love and faith in God. As the oft-used saying goes, "You can't give what you don't have." Most "on fire" young people need help in how to pray, how to read the Bible, and how to understand the sacraments so that they can mature in their newfound faith. They need practical instruction in relating as brothers and sisters, in serving others, in speaking of their experience, and in resolving conflict so that the witness of life matches their words.

---

3. Young people need to be trained in leadership.

Most youths are used to following, especially following the crowd. An evangelizer needs to lead. They need training in how to share their faith with confidence rather than with fear. They must be taught how to listen to their friends' concerns without being judgmental and how to invite their friends to turn to Christ. They need support in taking a positive stand on issues that affect youths such as chastity, honesty in school and work, and resistance to peer pressures.

---

4. Young people who evangelize will need us to serve as a resource for them as they uncover other youths who are experiencing personal difficulties.

My experience has been that as you begin sharing God's love and mercy with young people, they begin sharing their personal struggles with you. Youth evangelizers need to know where to turn when another youth shares that he or she has been abused or has attempted suicide. As the family system and the culture continue to deteriorate, young people's personal problems will continue to escalate. We must serve as a resource to our youth evangelizers so that they, in turn, can help youths in need to access the many support systems available to them.

Clearly, "youths evangelizing youths" does not get us adults off the hook. There is still a lot of work that we must do. But it is worth it. As we involve our young people in the work of evangelization, we will see them become more fully connected to Christ themselves. As you share your faith, your faith deepens. As young people do the work of the Church, they become more interested in the work of the Church. One of the things I never grow tired of hearing is a young person who tells me how excited he was as he shared his faith with another and suddenly realized, "God used me!"

Mark Bercham
National Evanglization Teams
West St. Paul, Minnesota

Integrating Youths into the Parish

When we gather as community, we include newly baptized infants, energetic children, searching adolescents, emerging young adults, adults at all stages, and seniors, who have had a longer experience of life's joys and struggles. We include families that take on a wide variety of shapes and sizes, yet each brings a real understanding of the domestic and larger Church.

Our youths are a treasured part of our Church and have much to give to the faith community, as well as a strong need to discover our rich heritage. As our young people live the faith and share the story of Christ, they become living witness to the dignity and power of our Lord's love in their lives and in our world.

Vatican II spoke of an image of Church as the "people of God." In the United States, our "people of God" consists of African Americans, Asians, Europeans, Hispanics, Native Americans, and all the historical, religious, and cultural traditions that define who we are and what we believe. As we integrate young people into parish life, we must be particularly sensitive and inclusive, therefore reinforcing Paul's instruction to the Colossians:

> Stop lying to one another, since you have taken off the old self with its practices and have put on the new self, which is being renewed, for knowledge, in the image of its creator. Here there is not Greek and Jew, circumcision and uncircumcision, barbarian, Scythian, slave, free; but Christ is all and in all (Col 3:9-11).

There are many young people who have not yet gained an awareness of their rich heritage.

As members of our community, they must be invited into a growing understanding and experience of building God's kingdom. Our youths need to discover the stories of faith of those who came before them, while realizing the living gospel that they bring into the world.

Today's youth culture sets young people apart from other age groups.

Their music, styles of clothing, and forms of entertainment speak specifically to them, and the mixed messages change quickly. However, when young people are asked about the things most important to them, they often speak of family, friends, acceptance, believing in God, and helping others.

Parish youth ministry can provide continuous opportunities for our youths to sort things out and determine how to integrate their faith into all areas of their lives.

The ministry setting involves loving adults who are present to walk with our youths as they learn to differentiate between that which is good and that which is harmful or destructive. Within ministry, young people learn that they are invited and needed to minister to each other.

These youths developed belief statements that spoke powerfully of their desire and willingness to minister to each other. Speaking about sexuality, the delegates asserted that "youth ministry is essential to give teens the spiritual direction and empowerment needed in a society that does not support Christian values and beliefs." Youth ministry must be an opportunity for our young people to learn and experience the gospel value of serving others.

Perhaps, in the past, we have decided that our young people would run a booth or clean up at the parish festival. Maybe they were baby-sitters on Sunday morning or for parish functions. Instead, we need to help our young people identify their gifts and invite them to use those gifts for the larger community. Maybe their gift is baby-sitting or working the parish festival, but it might also be teaching, liturgical music, art work, justice work, creative writing, or many other possibilities. Every young person has a special talent, and we need to think creatively about their using that talent to minister in the Church. An exit interview for confirmation candidates would be a wonderful time and place to discuss talents that surfaced during the confirmation journey and to ask candidates to share their talents in the future.

While acknowledging that most age groups are most comfortable with people of similar ages, we nevertheless need to recognize the value and dignity of people of every age. This means breaking down the stereotypes and fears that often surface concerning the young and the old. Young people live and operate in a world of relationships. Their willingness to reach out and build friendships is a valuable gift that invites and reminds the Church of the importance of getting to know others when building community.

Year after year, I have seen young people minister to and be touched by God through the lives of young and old alike. Many parishes have special liturgies for the anointing of the sick. Consider having young people greet and befriend each senior member by staying with them throughout the liturgy. When the celebrant anoints the senior member, the young person could also do hands on prayer, and all persons would experience God's powerful presence. Within the same liturgy, the homilist could invite the senior members to tell the young persons about God's story in their lives. Such opportunities give our young people the chance to reach beyond themselves in giving while receiving the treasures of our faith in word, story, and sacrament.

As they discover our Christian heritage, they take their rightful place as co-builders of God's kingdom and share the hope and good news of the gospel. Their presence in our families, schools, churches, and society is a living reminder that God is alive and working among us.

Greg Dobie Moser
Office of Youth Ministry
Columbus, Ohio

Reproducible Art

The artwork in this section has been created for use on bulletins, invitations, banners, posters, T-shirts, or in any way that your parish, school, or community finds helpful. Please feel free to trace, photocopy, enlarge, or reduce the artwork provided here and throughout the book and use it to enhance your celebration of World Youth Day 1992.

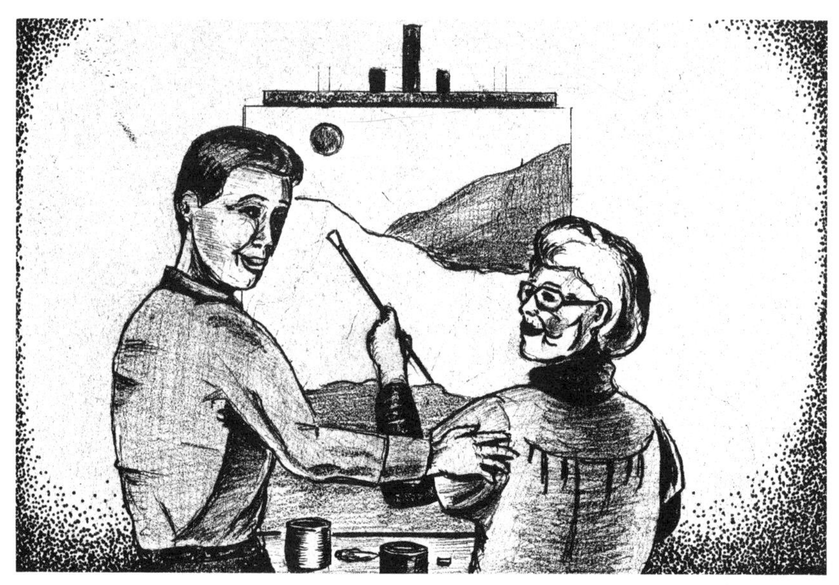

World Youth Day 1992
Live the Faith
Share the Story!

World Youth Day 1992
Live the Faith
Share the Story!

World Youth Day 1992
Live the Faith
Share the Story!

World Youth Day 1992
Live the Faith
Share the Story!

World Youth Day 1992
Live the Faith
Share the Story!

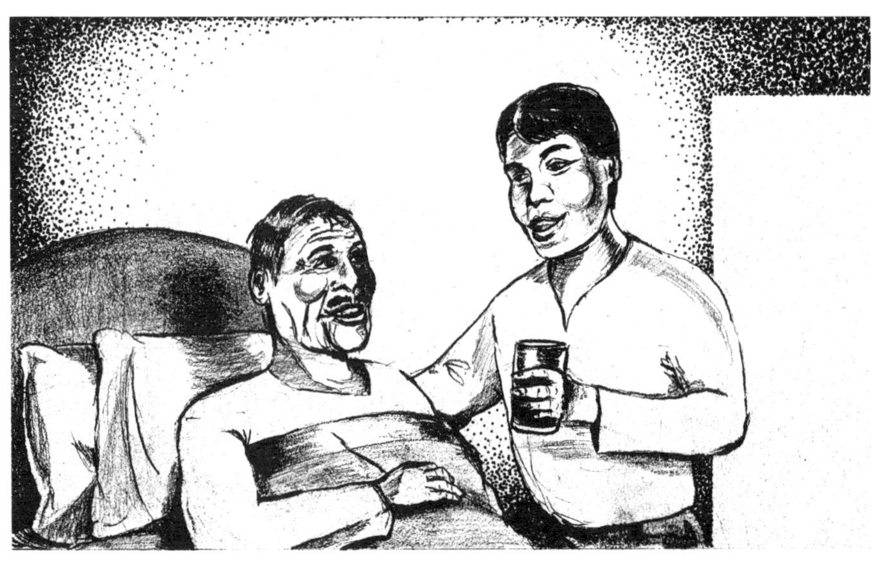

Evaluation

1. Please rank the usefulness of the 1992 booklet.

      1   2   3   4   5

   (not very useful)   (Excellent)

2. Using the scale below, please rate the effectiveness of the following components:

   1 = Not helpful
   2 = Somewhat helpful
   3 = Helpful
   4 = Very helpful

Reflecting on the Theme	1	2	3	4
A Blueprint for Celebrating World Youth Day	1	2	3	4
Parish and School Activities	1	2	3	4
A One-Day Retreat Model	1	2	3	4
Evangelization Training Session for Youths	1	2	3	4
An Adult Learning Session	1	2	3	4
Suggestions for Prayer and Worship	1	2	3	4
Stories of Young People	1	2	3	4
Youths as Evangelizers	1	2	3	4
Integrating Youths into the Parish	1	2	3	4
Message to Youth of the World (John Paul II)	1	2	3	4
Spanish-Language Section	1	2	3	4

3. What suggestions would you make for future World Youth Day books?

   ____

4. How did you celebrate World Youth Day 1992?

   ____

5. Please complete the following information.

   Name ____

   Position ____

   Address ____
           City   State   Zip Code

   Parish/Organization ____

   Telephone ____
           (area code)

Please return the completed form to:
Secretariat for Family, Laity, Women and Youth
National Conference of Catholic Bishops
3211 Fourth Street, N.E.
Washington, D.C. 20017-1194

Appendix 1

Message to the Youth of the World on the Occasion of VII World Youth Day 1992

Dear Young People,

1. The Lord blessed in a truly extraordinary way the VI World Youth Day, celebrated last August at the Shrine of Jasna Gora in Czestochowa.

As I announce for you the theme of the next Day, my thoughts go back to those wonderful moments, and I give thanks to Divine Providence for the spiritual fruits that have come from the World Meeting, not only for the Church, but for the whole of humanity.

How I wish that the breath of the Holy Spirit as we felt it in Czestochowa should be everywhere made present! During those unforgettable days, the Marian Shrine had become the cenacle of a new Pentecost, with its doors wide open towards the Third Millennium. Once again, the world was able to behold the Church, so youthful and so missionary, full of joy and hope.

I felt an immense happiness when I saw so many young people who, for the first time, had come together from the East and the West, from North and South, united by the Holy Spirit in the bond of prayer. We experienced an historic event whose immeasurable importance for salvation opened up a new stage in the path of evangelization where young people have an active part to play.

Here we are, then, for the VII World Youth Day 1992. As the theme for this year, I have chosen the words of Christ: "Go into all the world and preach the Gospel" (Mk 16:15). These words were addressed to the Apostles, but through the Church they reach every baptized person. It is easy to see that this theme is closely related to that of last year. The same Spirit who has made us sons and daughters of God, urges us on to evangelization. The Christian vocation implies, indeed, a mission.

In the light of the missionary mandate entrusted to us by Christ, emerge more clearly the meaning and the importance of the World Youth Days in the Church. By participating in these realities, the young people mean to confirm and strengthen their personal "yes" to Christ and to his Church. In the words of the prophet Isaish, they repeat: "Here I am! Send Me" (Is 6:8). This was precisely the meaning of the Rite of Sending which took place at Czestochowa when I handed lighted candles to some of your representatives, inviting all the young people to bear the Light of Christ into the world. Yes, at Jasna Gora—on the "Bright Mountain"—the Holy Spirit made a light shine forth, as sign of hope for the Church and for all of humankind.

2. The Church, of her nature, is a missionary community (cf. "Ad Gentes," n. 2). She lives constantly in the tension of the missionary thrust that she received from the Holy Spirit on the day of Pentecost: "You will receive power when the Holy Spirit comes upon you, and then you will be my wit- nesses" (Acts 1:8). The Holy Spirit is, indeed, the agent of the whole ecclesial mission (cf. *Redemptoris Missio*, III).

Once again, the world was able to behold the Church, so youthful and so missionary, full of joy and hope.

The Christian vocation has therefore a forward thrust, towards apostolate, towards evangelization, towards mission. Every baptized person is called by Christ to become his apostle in each one's daily environment and in the world: "As the Father has sent me, even so I send you" (Jn 20:21). Through his Church, Christ entrusts to you the fundamental mission of communicationg to others the gift of salvation, and he invites you to share in the building up of his Kingdom. He chooses you, in spite of each one's limitations, because he loves you and trusts you. This love of Christ, this unconditional love, must be the very soul of your apostolate, according to the words of St. Paul: "The love of Christ urges me on" (2 Cor 5:14).

To be Christ's disciples is not a private matter. On the contrary, the gift of faith must be shared with others.

To be Christ's disciples is not a private matter. On the contrary, the gift of faith must be shared with others. That is why the same Apostle writes: "If I preach the Gospel, that gives me no ground for boasting. Necessity is laid upon me. Woe to me if I do not preach the Gospel!" (1 Cor 9:16). Do not forget, moreover, that faith is strengthened and grows precisely when it is given to others (cf. Redemp*toris Missio,* n. 2).

3. "Go into all the world." The mission lands in which you are called to work are not necessarily located in distant countries; they can be found anywhere in the world, even in your daily environments. In countries with a more long-standing Christian tradition, it is urgently necessary today to give prominence to the proclamation of Jesus through a new evangelization. The multitude of those who do not know Christ, or who know little about him, is indeed still widely spread. There are many who have been caught in the mechanisms of secularism and religious indifference and have drifted away (cf. *Christifideles Laici,* n. 4).

Even the world of youth, my dear young people, is a mission territory for the Chruch today. Everyone is familiar with the problems that torment youthful environments: the decline of values, doubt, consumerism, drugs, crime, eroticism, and so forth. But, at the same time, there lives in every young person a great thirst for God, even if this is at times hidden behind an attitude of indifference or even of hostility. How many young people, astray and dissatistied, went to Czestochowa in order to give a deeper and decisive meaning to their own lives! How many came from afar—not only geographically—even without being baptized! I am convinced that for the lives of many young people the meeting at Czestochowa was a form of "evangelical preparation"; for some, it even marked an essential turning point, the occasion for an authentic conversion.

The harvest is abundant! And yet, while there are so many young people in search of Christ, the apostles capable of proclaiming him with credibility are still few in number. There is need of so many priests, teachers and educators in the faith; but there is also need of young people with a missionary spirit, for "the young should become the first apostles of the young, in direct contact with them, exercising the apostolate by themselves, among themselves" (*Apostolicam Actuositatem,* n. 12). That is a basic principle of education in faith. That, then, is your great task!

The world of today presents many challenges to your ecclesial commitment. In particular, the collapse of the Marxist system in the countries of Central and Eastern Europe and, as a consequence, the opening of many countries to the proclamation of Christ, constitute a new sign of the times, to which the Church is called to make an adequate response. In the same way, the Church is seeking ways to overcome the barriers of various kinds that still exist in many other countries. There is an absolute need of the drive and the enthusiasm which you, dear young people, are able to offer to the Church.

4. "Preach the Gospel." To proclaim Christ means above all to be witnesses to him by one's life. This is the simplest form of evangelization, and at the same time, the most effective, that you have at your disposal. It consists in showing the visible presence of Christ in one's own existence, through daily commitment and conformity with the Gospel in every concrete choice. Today the world needs above all credible witnesses. You, dear young people, who have such love for authenticity in persons, and who almost instinctively condemn every kind of hypocrisy are able to offer Christ a witness that is transparent and sincere.

The harvest is abundant! And yet, while there are so many young people in search of Christ, the apostles capable of proclaiming him with credibility are still few in number.

Bear witness then, to your faith, also through your commitment in the world. The disciple of Christ is never a passive and indifferent observer of events. On the contrary, he or she feels responsible for the transformation of social, political, economic and cultural reality.

To preach, moreover, which means precisely to proclaim, is to become a bearer to others of the Word of salvation. Many people reject God through ignorance. There is, indeed, a great deal of ignorance about the Christian faith; but there is also a deep desire to listen to the Word of God. And faith is born of listening. St. Paul writes: "How are they to believe in him of whom they have never heard? And how are they to hear without a preacher?" (Rom 10:14). To preach the Word of God is not a matter only for priests

or religious, but also for you. You must have the courage to speak of Christ in your families and in your place of study, work or recreation, moved by the same fervor as the Apostles, when they declared: "We cannot but speak of what we have seen and heard" (Acts 4:20). Neither must you be silent! There are places and situations to which you alone can bring the seed of the Word of God.

Do not be afraid to propose Christ to those who do not yet know him. Christ is the true and the most complete answer to all the questions concerning man and human destiny. Without him, the human being remains an unsolved puzzle. Have the courage, then, to propose Christ! This must, of course, be done with due respect for each one's freedom of con-

science, but it must be done (cf. *Redemptoris Missio*, n. 39). To help a brother or a sister to discover Christ, the Way, the Truth and the Life (cf. Jn 14:6), is a genuine act of love for one's neighbor.

Speaking of God, today, is not an easy task. There are many times when you come up against a wall of indifference, and even a certain hostility. How often you will be tempted to repeat with the Prophet Jeremiah: "Ah, Lord God! Behold, I do not know how to speak, for I am only a youth." But God always replies: "Do not say, I am only a youth, for to all to whom I send you, you shall go" (Jér 1:6-7). So, do not be discouraged, for you are never alone. Our Lord will not fail to accompany you, as he promised: "Know that I am with you always, yes, to the end of time" (Mt 28:20).

5. "Go into all the world and preach the Gospel." The theme of the VII World Youth Day invites you also to look at the history of the peoples, especially at the history of their evangelization.

In some cases, this is a very ancient history; in others, on the contrary, it is a recent history. But what is wonderful is the dynamism with which the younger Churches grow in faith, enriching the spiritual heritage of the whole of the universal Church.

On the occasion of this Day, beloved young people of the whole world, I invite you to reflect, in the light of faith, on the figures of the apostles and missionaries who were the first to raise the Cross of Christ in your countries. Try to take from their example the zeal and courage to face up better to the challenges of our times.

In gratitude for the gift of faith that they brought to the peoples, be willing personally to assume responsibility for the heritage of the Cross of Christ which you are called to transmit to the future generations.

At this point, I want to address a special word of encouragement to the young people of the Latin American Continent, where the V Centenary of the first evangelization will be celebrated this year. This event, of great importance for the whole Church, is for you an occasion to thank the Lord for the faith he has given you, and to renew your commitment with regard to the challenges of the new evangelization, on the threshold of the Third Millennium.

6. The publication of this Message inaugurates the path of spiritual preparation for the celebration of the next World Youth Day, which will gather you around your Bishops on Palm Sunday.

The ordinary character of the celebration must not, however, imply less commitment. On the contrary, I invite you, the youth and those responsible for pastoral work among youth, as well as the leaders of movements, associations and ecclesial communities, to make an even greater effort, so that this "path" may become a real school of evangelization and apostolic formation.

I hope that many young men and young women, inspired by sincere zeal for the apostolate, will want to consecrate their lives to Christ and to his Church, as priests, as religious brothers and sisters, or as lay people who are ready to leave their own country and go where the laborers are becoming few in Christ's vineyard. Listen, then, carefully to the vioce of the Lord who, today, is still calling you, as he called Peter and Andrew: "Follow me, and I will make you fishers of men" (Mt 4:19).

As the year 2000 draws near, the Church feels the need for a renewed missionary thrust and, precisely for this, she places great hope in you, beloved young people. Do not forget every day to thank the Holy Spirit, who continues to kindle so many fires of apostolic commitment in the Church of today. Parish communities that are alive and dynamic are a most fertile ground for this commitment, as are also the associations, movements and new communities that are growing and spreading with such a wealth of charisms, especially among the youth. This is a new breath from the Holy Spirit, as a gift for our times. How I should like this breath to enter into the life of each one of you.

I entrust to Mary, Queen of Apostles, the celebration of the World Youth Day 1992. May she teach you that, to bring Jesus to others, it is not necessary to perform extraordinary deeds; it is enough simply to have a heart brimful with love for God and for one's brothers and sisters, a love that urges us to share the inestimable treasures of faith, hope and charity.

All along the way of your preparation for the VII World Youth Day, may you be accompainied, beloved young people, by my special Apostolic Blessing.

From the Vatican, November 24, 1991, Solemnity of Our Lord Jesus Christ, King of the Universe.

---

† John Paul II

Appendix 2

WORLD YOUTH DAY 1993
PAPAL YOUTH MEETING

The Holy Father has once again invited young people (youths and young adults) from around the world to meet with him for several days of catechesis, reconciliation, and prayer. This meeting in August 1993 will take place for the first time in the United States.

This presents us with a wonderful opportunity to not only welcome youths from around the world but to make a special effort to welcome and reach out to young people in the United States, thereby making this meeting with the Holy Father a celebration of a year of youth evangelization and outreach.

To prepare for the International celebration of World Youth Day 1993, we invite each parish, school, and catholic organization to designate individuals—volunteer or paid—to work with the entire parish or school community to evangelize youths who are not a part of our community, to train other youths to be evangelizers, and to reach out to those who are baptized but are not present in our communities. World Youth Day 1992 can be the beginning of this year of evangelization and outreach to young people, culminating in the meeting with the Holy Father in August 1993.

To help us prepare for and participate in this year of outreach and evangelization some suggestions are listed below. These are in addition to those already found in this manual. More detailed information will be available later in the year.

Using This Year's Theme

The theme for 1992, *Live the Faith, Share the Story!* can be used beyond this year's celebration. As we begin the year of evangelization and outreach, the two-fold focus of putting on an attitude of Christ and witnessing to family and friends can serve us well. This theme challenges those young people who are already baptized and participating to become today's apostles; to share the message of Christ with those at home, in school, and at work. For those young people who do not know Jesus or who are alienated from the Church, we must make a special effort to share the story with them. In late 1992, as is his custom, the Holy Father will issue a *Message to the Youth of the World on the Occasion of the VIII World Youth Day.* In that message, he will set forth the theme for the 1993 celebration.

Getting Started

The following suggestions are offered to help you in getting started. More detailed information will be available in the summer/fall of 1992.

- Obtain a copy of *Called to Be Witnesses and Storytellers: Catholic Youth Outreach and Evangelization* (National Federation for Catholic Youth Ministry; 3900-A Harewood Road, N.E.; Washington, D.C. 20017); and a copy of *A Vision of Youth Ministry* (USCC Office for Publishing and Promotion Services; 3211 Fourth Street, N.E.; Washington, D.C. 20017; phone: 1-800-235-USCC).

- Begin an initiation process (RCIA) for adolescents and young adults if your parish does not have one in place.

- Train interested and dynamic young people to be outreach workers (evangelists).

- Sponsor special "Come and See" and "Welcome Home" evenings and celebrations for those young people who have left the Church or who do not know Jesus Christ.

- Work to integrate young people into all parish ministries and activities.

- Develop a parish focus that welcomes all persons to participate in the life of the community.

- Develop Christian service projects so that young people can comprehend their faith as one that is lived daily by actions and words.

- Use the theme *Live the Faith, Share the Story!* in youth-group meetings, religious education classes, scout meetings, and on retreats.

- Invite adult organizations to participate by asking them to discuss the theme and to envision how they can become mentors to young people in the parish, school, or community.

Preparations for World Youth Day 1993 should be intergenerational, involving youths with their families and other adults within the community.

This is not meant to be something JUST for young people but for the whole parish. Invite the parish to make as its priority and focus the welcoming, participation, and formation of youths. Below is a suggested yearlong process, which can be adapted easily for the school calendar:

The success of this yearlong process is dependent on a parish or a school investing time and energy in a total youth, young adult, or campus ministry program that has the support of the pastor, the parish council, and the parish staff or, in a school, the support of the principal, the teachers and staff, and the PTA.

Planning Schedule for World Youth Day 1993

October 1992

— World Youth Day 1992 Celebration

November—December 1992

— Planning and Recruitment
— Training of Youths and Adults as Evangelists

January 1993

— Celebration to Begin Year of Evangelization and Outreach

February—June 1993

— Outreach and Evangelization
— Enrollment of Youths Wishing to Be Baptized or to Profess the Catholic Faith in the Parish Christian Initiation Process

August 1993

— Papal Meeting and Catechesis with Young People

Easter 1994

— Full Initiation into the Catholic Faith for Those Enrolled during the 1993 Evangelization Program

Contenido

¡Vive la Fe, Comparte la Historia!

¡Actitud! ¡Todo el mundo tiene cierta actitud! La actitud refleja lo que pensamos de nosotros mismos, de nuestro mundo y de los demás seres humanos. La manera en que nos relacionamos con Dios también depende de nuestra actitud.

Las lecturas para el Día Mundial de la Juventud mencionan actitudes diferentes. En la lectura de Eclesiástico nos enteramos de la actitud divina: Dios oye el grito de los pobres . . . Dios no tiene preferencias . . . la oración de los que se acercan a Dios con humildad llega al cielo. La actitud de Pablo en 2 Timoteo es de confianza porque el Señor está con él— él ha hecho su trabajo: "He terminado mi carrera, siempre fiel a la fe."

La lectura del Evangelio presenta dos actitudes opuestas. El fariseo que orgullosamente se jacta de su justificación ante Dios como resultado de sus buenas obras, y el colector de impuestos que reconoce sus faltas y se presenta ante Dios con humildad, buscando misericordia. Este pasaje nos recuerda que nuestra actitud y la actitud de la sociedad no corresponden a la actitud de Cristo; que lo que a veces pensamos es el camino a la santidad, no lo es; que lo que proclamamos en alta voz como el mejor camino, no lo es. El reto es ser receptivo a la presencia de Dios en nuevas maneras de pensar y actuar; que los que pensamos son los menos importantes son los que nos pueden enseñar más. ¿Cuál es nuestra actitud hacia Dios y hacia nuestra fe?

La celebración del Día Mundial de la Juventud de 1992 nos presenta la oportunidad de reflexionar sobre nuestra actitud hacia Dios, hacia su pueblo y hacia nuestra fe. ¡El 1992 nos desafía a entender nuestra herencia cristiana, a revestirnos con la actitud de Cristo, y a compartir la historia cristiana! Nuevamente, ¿cuál es nuestra actitud hacia nuestra fe? ¿La escondemos para nosotros mismos como si fuera una experiencia personal privada? o, ¿la sacamos a relucir para que brille ante los demás? Vivir nuestra fe exige que compartamos su mensaje porque lo que consideramos ser valioso nunca lo guardamos en secreto pero siempre lo compartimos con los demás.

En su mensaje a los jóvenes del mundo en 1990, el Santo Padre desafió a los jóvenes a examinar su actitud hacia la fe. Les pidió que fuesen los nuevos apóstoles para esta década. Hoy, en 1992, el Papa Juan Pablo II nuevamente confronta nuestra actitud. Le pide a los jóvenes que se den cuenta que tienen mucho que dar a la Iglesia y a la sociedad:

> Ustedes tienen que poseer la valentía de hablar sobre Cristo a sus familiares y en sus ambientes de trabajo, estudio o diversión. La energía y el entusiasmo que ustedes, muy apreciados jóvenes, pueden ofrecer a la Iglesia son indispensables. Ser discípulos de Cristo no es un asunto privado . . . al contrario, el don de la fe tiene que ser compartido.

Vivir nuestra fe exige que compartamos su mensaje porque lo que consideramos ser valioso nunca lo guardamos en secreto pero siempre lo compartimos con los demás.

El Santo Padre nos dice además que los jóvenes están llamados a ser misioneros entre sus familiares y amigos:

> La juventud católica está llamada a mostrar con su estilo de vida y sus decisiones que la fe es una respuesta factible a la indiferencia y a la hostilidad. Los cristianos, no importa su edad, tienen que tener la valentía

de "presentar a Cristo" a todos lo que buscan significado en sus vidas. Vayan por todo el mundo y proclamen las Buenas Nuevas.

¡Revístanse de la actitud de Cristo!

¡En otras palabras el Santo Padre desafía a los jóvenes para que actúen! Él los desafía para que vivan la fe y compartan la historia.

Vive la fe

¡"Revístanse" de la actitud de Cristo! ¿Cuál es la actitud de Cristo? Es una actitud de humildad, misericordia y cuidado por la creación de Dios. El pecado del fariseo del Evangelio es que estaba orgulloso de su bondad y virtud en vez de presentarse ante Dios y de confiar en su perdón y misericordia. El fariseo lo podía hacer todo. No necesitaba el perdón de Dios, ni su ayuda. El 1992 nos presenta la oportunidad de reflexionar en nuestra necesidad de recibir la misericordia de Dios y su perdón por nuestras acciones erradas como individuos o como pueblo: en la manera en que nos relacionamos con nuestro medio ambiente; en la manera en que tratamos a los demás; en la manera en que maltratamos a nuestro cuerpo por medio de las drogas y el alcohol. Esta actitud de humildad es también el reconocimiento de la necesidad de "revestirnos" con la actitud de Cristo.

Comparte la Historia

Sean evangelizadores de la familia, los amigos, la sociedad. Ustedes los jóvenes, como miembros plenos de la comunidad, son llamados a ser señales de la presencia amorosa de Dios en este mundo. Mientras que la sabiduría tradicional presenta a los jóvenes como recipientes de la sabiduría de los adultos—"Cuando los adolescentes crezcan entonces podrán contribuir algo a la Iglesia y a la sociedad"—la juventud es capaz de contribuir a sus comunidades. La juventud puede asumir el desafío de ser instrumentos de Dios en el mundo: en la familia, en la escuela, en el trabajo, y en la iglesia. La juventud tiene un llamado especial a ser señales del amor de Cristo, especialmente entre los demás jóvenes. Los adultos deben escuchar y aprender de la juventud y los que han trabajado con los jóvenes dan testimonio de esta realidad. Caminamos juntos en el peregrinar de la fe, respetándonos, dando y recibiendo mutuamente.

Paul K. Henderson
Director Asociado del
Secretariado para la Familia,
los Laicos y la Juventud
Conferencia Nacional de
Obispos Católicos
Washington, D.C.

Descubriendo el Patrimonio Cristiano de Nuestros Santos

Planeen un día para celebrar los santos de los diferentes países representados en su parroquia. Este día sería preparado por los jóvenes de la parroquia y consistiría de una recepción en el salón parroquial o afuera.

Pongan una mesa para cada cultura que se vaya a representar. Las mesas pueden incluir altares para los santos de ese país y pueden ser decorados con fotos, flores y velas.

También pueden tener un cartelón con la vida del santo o la manera en que ese santo vivió el espíritu de Cristo. Pueden incluir información acerca de la cultura de donde viene el santo. Otras cosas que se pueden incluir son mapas del país, fotos e historias de familias que han emigrado a los Estados Unidos que forman parte de la parroquia. Se pueden ofrecer galletas, panes, y dulces originarios de ese país para que todos los disfruten.

Después de las misas del Día Mundial de la Juventud inviten a los feligreses a participar en la celebración y a aprender más acerca de la variedad de personas que han mantenido vivo nuestro patrimonio cristiano.

Rezando por Nuestros Jóvenes

Invite a la parroquia a rezar por los jóvenes durante la semana antes del Día Mundial de la Juventud. Distribuyan estampas con la oración y pidan a los feligreses que la recen todos los días.

- **Primero:** Inviten a los jóvenes de la comunidad a preparar un diseño para la estampa.

- **Segundo:** Escojan o escriban una oración para la estampa. Mándenla a imprimir.

- **Tercero:** Distribuyan la estampa a la comunidad el domingo antes del Día Mundial de la Juventud. Pidan a los sacerdotes que expliquen por qué se están dando las estampas. Pongan un anuncio en el boletín parroquial. El anuncio puede decir algo así:

Les invitamos a rezar por los jóvenes del mundo. El Papa Juan Pablo II y los líderes de nuestra Iglesia han designado el próximo domingo como Día Mundial de la Juventud. El tema de este año es: Vive la fe . . . Comparte la historia. Este domingo estamos distribuyendo estampas con una oración especial. Les pedimos que recen por todos los jóvenes del mundo una vez al día.

- **Cuarto:** Dénle las gracias a la comunidad durante el Día Mundial de la Juventud por haber rezado por los jóvenes. Durante la misa incluyan la oración que está en la estampa.

Se puede usar esta oración:

Día Mundial de la Juventud de 1992
Vive la Fe, Comparte la Historia

Padre Santísimo,
oramos en solidaridad con todo tu pueblo por los jóvenes del mundo.

Bendícelos hoy,
para que estén salvos de la violencia,
las drogas, la pobreza.

Llénalos del Espíritu de Cristo
para que se conviertan en signo de tu amor,
y líderes en esperanza, justicia y paz.

Manténlos unidos en tu amor.

Te pedimos esto por Jesucristo y por nuestra Señora, la Reina del Cielo. Amén.

Modelos de Fe Hoy Día—Viendo el Espíritu de Cristo

- Presenten el tema del Día Mundial de la Juventud. Dividan al grupo en grupos pequeños de tres o cuatro. Que cada grupo pequeño escoja una persona contemporánea que sea un ejemplo de vida cristiana. Que cada grupo prepare una presentación acerca de la persona. La persona puede estar viva o muerta: la Madre Teresa de Calcutta o el Arzobispo Oscar Romero de El Salvador. Las presentaciones pueden incluir música, cartelones, transparencias, vídeos, presentaciones teatrales u otras formas de expresión artística. Permitan una o dos semanas para que los jóvenes preparen las presentaciones. Dependiendo del número de grupos que tengan estas presentaciones se pueden hacer todas juntas o en el curso de varias semanas, como al principio de las clases de educación religiosa o durante la junta de jóvenes.

Celebrando el Espíritu de Cristo en Nuestra Comunidad Joven

- **Primero:** Pidan a los jóvenes que reflexionen acerca de las maneras que como comunidad están viviendo el llamado de Cristo. Por ejemplo: ayudando a los pobres, cantando en las misas, dando clases de inglés u otras formas de servicio. Pueden tomar notas de lo que se comparte.

  Después que reflexionen acerca de que más podrían hacer por la comunidad como grupo o como individuos. Se pueden desarrollar metas de estas ideas para el próximo año. Por ejemplo: se necesita trabajar más para los pobres de la parroquia; los jóvenes pueden adoptar una o más familias que necesitan nuestra ayuda durante este año; u organizar una colecta de ropa antes del inicio de la escuela, la Navidad y la Pascua.

  Mientras más desarrollada esté la idea más probabilidad hay de que se lleve acabo el proyecto.

  ✛ ✛ ✛ ✛ ✛ ✛ ✛

- **Segundo:** Que se tomen fotos de las diferentes actividades donde los jóvenes responden al Espíritu de Cristo. Pongan las fotos en un cartelón describiendo lo que los jóvenes están haciendo en la comunidad. También pueden incluir sus metas para el próximo año, sin dar detalles específicos, como por ejemplo, el nombre de la familia que piensan ayudar.

  El cartelón se coloca en un lugar donde la comunidad lo pueda ver durante el mes de octubre o noviembre.

- **Tercero:** Al final del año se hace una evaluación para ver cuántas metas se alcanzaron, y cuál fue el efecto de sus acciones. Desarrollen metas nuevas para el próximo año.

Viviendo Nuestro Patrimonio Cristiano de Justicia y Servicio

- **Primero:** Junten a un grupo para identificar las necesidades de la comunidad, concentrándose en especial en los más humildes. Escojan una área de necesidad dónde puedan hacer no solamente caridad directa, sino también acción social. Por ejemplo: asistencia a madres con niños pequeños (WICS). Pueden identificar quiénes son las mujeres en su parroquia que mantienen a sus hijos solas y ayudarlas con comida o ropa y también abogar a nivel social para más servicios para ellas y sus hijos.

- **Segundo:** Planeen una experiencia para dar caridad directa, como juntar comida o ropa y distribuirla a los pobres.

- **Tercero:** Estudien las causas de la pobreza a nivel social. Pidan a alguien que dé una explicación al grupo acerca de la 'opción preferencial por los pobre,' y los documentos de Medellín y Puebla, la teología de la liberación, la Pastoral de los Obispos Católicos de los Estados Unidos sobre la Economía. Es importante que nuestros jóvenes tengan la oportunidad de aprender acerca de la riqueza del patrimonio de justicia y paz que brota de la teología pastoral de Latinoamérica y de este país.

  ✛ ✛ ✛ ✛ ✛ ✛ ✛

- **Cuarto:** Planeen un proyecto de acción política, como escribir cartas a un senador sobre un asunto de importancia a la comunidad: el medio ambiente, el desempleo, la educación, asistencia médica, etc.

- **Quinto:** Junten al grupo una vez más para reflexionar acerca del efecto que tuvieron sus acciones caritativas y de interés social y político. Planeen que más podrían hacer como grupo.

Celebrando el Patrimonio de Fe de Nuestras Familias

- Pidan a los jóvenes que reflexionen acerca de los bienes espirituales que han recibido de sus familias, padres, madres, abuelas y abuelos, tías y tíos. Por ejemplo: De mi abuela aprendí a ser caritativa. De mi madre aprendí que Dios siempre nos ampara.

  - Que los jóvenes preparen una comida para sus padres y abuelos y otros familiares en agradecimiento de esos bienes espirituales que han recibido.

  - Que escriban o reciten poemas para los padres y abuelos (u otros) que expresen ese agradecimiento. Los jóvenes pueden explicar los bienes espirituales que han recibido de sus mayores. Esto podría ser hecho en drama u otra forma artística.

  - Que escojan como grupo a una o dos personas ancianas que todos consideren son modelos especiales de fe. Le pueden pedir que sea invitada(o) especial de la recepción. Pidan a un joven que dé una presentación especial acerca de esta persona dónde explique porque el grupo considera que esta persona es un modelo de fe para los jóvenes. Le pueden obsequiar con una placa, un pergamino, o con flores.

- Preparen tarjetas para cada padre, abuelo u otro familiar que diga:

  - En agradecimiento de la fe católica que me has dado. Que Dios Santísimo te bendiga hoy y siempre.

  - Que cada joven firme la tarjeta que va a enviar a sus padres, abuelos u otro familiar.

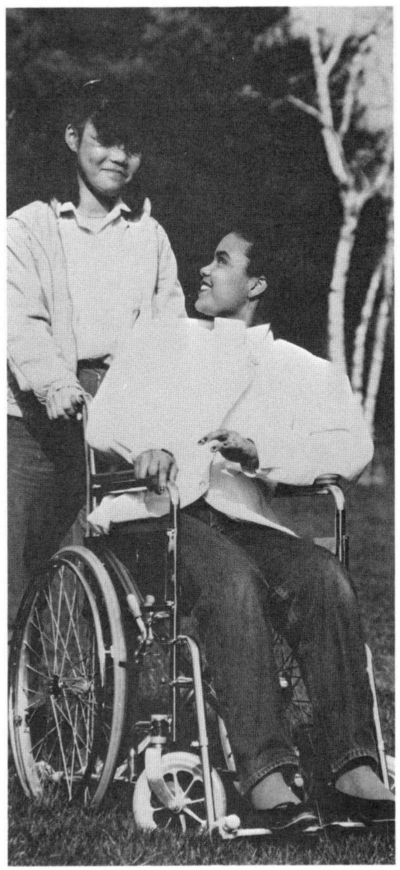

Descubriendo el Patrimonio de Fe de Nuestra Parroquia

- Junten a un grupo para estudiar la historia de su propia parroquia. Los jóvenes pueden trabajar con un asesor. Algunas áreas para estudiar son:

  - ¿Cómo y cuándo fue establecida la parroquia?

  - ¿Cómo fue seleccionado o adquirido el sitio?

  - ¿Cómo fue seleccionado el nombre?

  - ¿Cuál es la historia del santo patrón de la parroquia?

- Esto se puede hacer estudiando los archivos de la parroquia o la diócesis. Dependiendo de cuantos años ha estado en existencia la parroquia, los jóvenes podrían hablar con personas que ayudaron a establecer la parroquia o que conocen bien su historia. Una vez que se ha juntado la información los jóvenes pueden organizar una fiesta para el día del santo patrón de la parroquia. Pueden usar fotos antiguas, o los planos originales para darle a la comunidad una idea de como era la parroquia en el pasado. Se pueden celebrar las mañanitas, preparar pastel, piñatas u otras actividades tradicionales para el día del patrón.

Redescubriendo el Patrimonio de Nuestra Fe Popular

- Dividan a los jóvenes en grupos pequeños. Pidan a cada grupo que estudie una tradición católica, por ejemplo el rosario, Día de Muertos, o las posadas. ¿Cómo empezó esta tradición? ¿Por qué se empezó a practicar y por qué se practica hoy día? Dénle dos o más semanas de preparación a los grupos. Las presentaciones pueden incluir cartelones, transparencias, o cualquier otra forma de expresión artística. Cada grupo también puede preparar un evento donde se celebre esta tradición. Por ejemplo: Una posada, altares para el Día de Muertos, o la misa para los niños el Día de Reyes Magos. Con un poco de preparación pueden usar lo que han aprendido todo el año.

Celebrando el Día Mundial de la Juventud con la Comunidad Entera

- Junten a un grupo de jóvenes y adultos con tiempo para preparar la liturgia del día y la fiesta parroquial después. Usen las ideas dadas en este libro que les ayuden a celebrar debidamente la ocasión.

- Dividan al grupo en dos. Una parte para preparar la liturgia, la otra para preparar la fiesta.

La Liturgia

Si hay más de una misa en español escojan la misa que será dedicada a los jóvenes.

Lean las lecturas para la misa del día de jóvenes. Basado en las lecturas escojan las canciones; escriban las peticiones; escojan jóvenes para leer las lecturas, llevar las ofrendas, proveer la hospitalidad para la misa, servir en el coro y servir de acólitos. Pueden pedirle a los jóvenes que entren en procesión, o que hagan una valla. También pueden recibir una bendición especial del sacerdote. Pueden presentar una de las lecturas dramáticamente, o usar una de las presentaciones que han preparado para una de las otras actividades de este libro. También pueden combinar actividades. Por ejemplo: Hacer tres presentaciones cortas, una acerca de un santo, una acerca de una persona que es modelo de fe como el Arzobispo Romero, y una acerca de un joven o anciano de la parroquia. Que la misa incluya música alegre, color, y drama.

La Fiesta

Que el segundo grupo decida como se puede celebrar el Día Mundial de la Juventud después de las misa. Pueden usar una de las ideas incluida en este libro, o pueden planear una fiesta, que incluya comida, música, baile y combinaciones de las ideas presentadas en este libro.

Descubriendo el Patrimonio Católico en Nuestra Comunidad

- Junten a un grupo para estudiar cómo vino la fe católica a la comunidad originalmente. Los jóvenes pueden trabajar con un asesor. Algunas de las áreas para estudiar son: ¿Cómo y cuándo se estableció la primera parroquia o misión en nuestra área? Por ejemplo, en Los Ángeles la primera misión fue San Gabriel.

  - ¿Quiénes fueron las personas que tomaron parte en ese primer esfuerzo?
  - ¿Cuáles fueron algunos de los obstáculos?
  - ¿Cuáles fueron algunas de las consecuencias positivas y negativas de nuestra venida?

- Usen los archivos diocesanos y las bibliotecas. Encuentren fotos o pinturas del área cuando se estableció la Iglesia en esa comunidad.

- Que preparen una presentación que se pueda hacer a otros jóvenes, a la comunidad entera o a un grupo de niños. Usen fotos, dibujos, transparencias, drama, canciones o cualquier otra forma de expresión artística.

Maria Elena Cardeña
Oficina para Ministerio de Jóvenes
Arquidiócesis de Los Ángeles

Adaptada de la actividad originalmente en el inglés desarrollado por Tom East, Oficina de Ministerio Juvenil, Los Ángeles.

Retiro Juvenil de Un Día

El tema del día: "Dios tiene algo preparado para mí"
(cfr. 2 Tm 4:8)

Aquí presentamos los temas que se van a desarrollar durante el día. Otros elementos prácticos, sobre todo de organización, quedan a la discreción de quienes organizan el día de retiro. Ofrecemos, sin embargo, un esquema para el horario.

9:00 a.m. **Ambientación (coro o canciones grabadas)**

9:30 a.m. **Oración inicial: Daniel 3:52-88 (dos coros)**

10:00 a.m. **Primer tema: *"Ponle color a tus sueños"***

Desarrollo del tema

- ◆ La realidad en la que vives (país de origen; situación económica; relación con tus padres y demás miembros de la familia; ambiente en el que has crecido, etc.).

- ◆ ¿Cuáles son tus sueños e inquietudes?; ¿qué te gustaría ser en la vida?; ¿cuáles son tus planes para el futuro?

- ◆ ¿Con qué aptitudes, talentos, cuentas?; ¿qué sabes o te gusta hacer?; ¿para qué tienes facilidad (música, deporte, literatura, etc.)?

- ◆ La exposición del tema, juntamente con la participación activa de los jóvenes, no deberá exceder una hora.

- ◆ Al concluir, el expositor, puede aclarar el origen de todas esas inquietudes y preguntas que los jóvenes tienen o se hacen, así como referirse al Autor de los talentos que poseen.

11:15 a.m. **Descanso (se podrían usar cantos de ambientación)**

11:45 a.m. **Segundo tema: *"Por qué mis sueños son grises"***

Desarrollo del tema

- ◆ Existe pobreza, violencia, injusticia, discriminación, incomprensión, envidia, odio, enfermedades, limitaciones físicas o intelectuales, desajustes culturales, conflictos emocionales, etc. que condicionan la vida del joven y que influyen en su comportamiento.

- ◆ Ocasiones en las que han predominado estos aspectos negativos en la vida de los jóvenes; experiencias personales del mal: de todo aquello que impide al joven desarrollarse o realizarse según sus deseos o sueños; de todo aquello que constituye un obstáculo para realizar un plan en su vida. (Se puede aprovechar este momento para hacer un recorrido de los Diez Mandamientos. Se puede también hacer una tabla comparativa de los valores para las diferentes generaciones).

- ◆ El tema no debe durar más de una hora y cuarto, incluida la participación activa de los jóvenes.

1:00 p.m. **Almuerzo y juegos**

3:15 p.m. **Tercer tema: *"Volver a soñar"***

Rito penitencial y confesiones

Lecturas sugeridas

- Parábola de los Talentos (Mt 25:14-30)
- Parábola del Hijo Pródigo (Lc 15:11-32)
- Parábola del Fariseo y el Publicano (Lc. 18:9-14)
- Efesios 4:17-30
- Salmo 50
- ◆ A la luz de la Palabra se pueden recordar los dos temas anteriores para llevar a los jóvenes hacia la idea de que es Dios quien los llama a ser alguien

en la vida ya que han sido creados a su imagen y semejanza y en sus manos está la obra del mismo Dios (Gn 1:26-27; Sal 8). El pecado, sin embargo, es el gran obstáculo que les impide realizar el plan de Dios en sus vidas.

- Mientras los jóvenes se confiesan se recomienda un clima de silencio y de oración. Se pueden promover actividades como hacer dibujos u oraciones sobre el tema del perdón y de la reconciliación.

4:30 p.m.	**Descanso (Se pueden usar cantos de ambientación)**
4:45 p.m.	**Cuarto tema: "Compartir mis sueños con los demás"**

Desarrollo del tema

- La experiencia del pecado ha hecho ver al joven lo que ha perdido (Hijo Pródigo), pero al mismo tiempo lo ha puesto de nuevo en camino: "Me levantaré y volveré a la casa de mi Padre." Recuerda la actitud del publicano que le merece el perdón. Los dones del padre (vestido nuevo, sandalias nuevas, anillo al dedo, la fiesta de bienvenida) significan lo mucho que vale el joven para su padre. La actitud del padre es un ejemplo para el adulto. En su silencio tiene mucho que decir a jóvenes y adultos. Hay adultos en quienes los jóvenes pueden confiar y de quienes pueden aprender.

- El camino de regreso no lo hace el joven solo. Otros— jóvenes y adultos—caminan con él. Algunos tienen un camino más largo que recorrer o van a necesitar ayuda en el camino. Se trata de los pobres, de los ignorantes, de los débiles, de los que sufren. El mismo Padre los está esperando también a ellos.

- Lo que el joven ha descubierto este día lo puede compartir con otros jóvenes que están pasando por situaciones semejantes a las que él ha pasado. A partir de hoy tiene una misión más en la vida: compartir sus sueños, nuevos sueños, sueños de vida, sueños de hijo que ha encontrado de nuevo la casa de su padre, sueños que han comenzado a realizarse por el hecho de haber recorrido ya parte del camino . . . Quizá existe alguien con quien el joven desea compartir sus sueños; quizá existan sueños que ahora podrán cumplirse después de esta experiencia positiva, después de este retiro. . . .

Sería bueno terminar con la celebración de la Eucaristía y, durante el ofertorio, se podrían ofrecer los "propósitos" o "compromisos", los sueños que los jóvenes quieran realizar.

6:00 p.m.	**Descanso, preparación para la Eucaristía. . . .**
6:30 p.m.	**Celebración de la Santa Misa**

- Renovación de las promesas del bautismo durante el Credo
- Ofrecimiento de "sueños" que se quieren logra

---

*Reverendo Miguel A. Villegas
Covina, California*

Servicio Litúrgico para el Día Mundial de la Juventud de 1992

Líder:

Iniciemos esta oración con un momento de silencio.

[*Pausa.*]

Ahora, manteniendo la oración en silencio, hacemos el gesto que nos marca a todos como cristianos.

[*Todos hacen la señal de la cruz muy despacio y deliberadamente.*]

Líder:

Casi todos aquí hemos usado una cámara fotográfica para retratar a los amigos, la familia, un lugar especial, una ocasión especial, un incidente cómico, o algo que queremos recordar. Sin embargo, más importante que la cámara es nuestra memoria que está llena de imágenes que hemos tomado con el lente de la mente. Yo los invito a que durante los próximos dos minutos traten de recordar una de esas imágenes de un padre, una abuela, una maestra, un amigo o amiga, un hermano o hermana o cualquier otra persona que te ayudó a descubrir algo del significado de la fe en Cristo.

[*Durante los momentos de reflexión se podría poner música de fondo apropiada que trate de la distancia entre las diferentes generaciones. Según el número de personas en el grupo, invite a cada persona a compartir su imagen con una o dos personas o con el grupo en-*tero. *Se concluye el intercambio con este oración.*]

Todos:
Oh Dios generoso,
te damos gracias por el regalo de
    aquellas personas
que nos han precedido en la fe.

Ellas nos han ayudado a apreciar
    tu bondad
y nos han dirigido hacia la
    verdad.

Nuestras reflexiones sobre estas
    personas especiales
nos recuerdan que somos
    responsables de pasar la fe a
    los demás,
especialmente a las generaciones
    futuras.

Que con tu gracia,
podamos dar testimonio de tu
    amorosa presencia
y del espíritu de Cristo, en cuyo
    nombre hacemos esta oración.

Amén.

CANTO

LECTURA

1 Corintios 1:3-9

ORACIÓN EN SILENCIO

LETANÍA DE GRACIAS

Señor, nuestros niños y jóvenes son una bendición:

Respuesta:
    Te damos gracias, Señor.

Por su entusiasmo por la vida . . .
  R/.

Por su inocencia y curiosidad . . .
  R/.

Por su deseo de aprender nuevas cosas . . .
  R/.

Por su impaciencia con palabras vacías . . .
  R/.

Por su cuestionamiento de la autoridad . . .
  R/.

Por su naciente liderazgo . . .
  R/.

Por su creatividad e imaginación . . .
  R/.

Por su amistad cariñosa . . .
  R/.

Por su deseo de servir a los demás . . .
  R/.

[*Se pueden añadir otras peticiones espontáneas.*]

Líder:

Los invito ahora a pensar en algún joven que necesite una palabra de ánimo, un abrazo cariñoso, un halago sincero, una palabra de agradecimiento, un oído receptivo, o sólo unos minutos de tu tiempo. Comprométete a cumplir tu intención y al hacerlo menciona en voz alta el primer nombre de esa persona. [*Los nombres se mencionan sin seguir un orden específico.*]

Líder:

Completando nuestra letanía de acción de gracias decimos la oración que Jesús nos enseñó: [*Todos dicen el Padre Nuestro . . .*]

Líder:

Dios amoroso,
de generación en generación
   has dado a tu Iglesia
testigos de tu fidelidad y amor.

En este Día Mundial de la
   Juventud,
oramos para que nuestros
   jóvenes se conviertan en
   nuevos apóstoles de las
   generaciones futuras,
y sean fieles testigos de tu
   presencia entre nosotros.

Que cada uno de nosotros se
   llene del espíritu de los
   discípulos
y crezca en actitudes de
   servicio, humildad y
   perseverancia.

Te lo pedimos por Cristo,
   nuestro Señor.

Amén.

CANTO

"Mi Pequeñita Luz, la Dejaré Brillar"

Bendición del Día Mundial de la Juventud

Señor, nuestros niños y jóvenes
   son una bendición tuya.

En este Día Mundial de la
   Juventud,
te pedimos que los bendigas de
   manera especial.

Si están desanimados y
   desengañados
bendícelos con nuevo
   entusiasmo por la vida.

Dale amistades sinceras y
   verdaderas,
que les ayuden a descubrir las
   alegrías de tu creación y a
   permanecer fuertes cuando
   se enfrenten a las presiones
   de la vida.

Bendice sus experiencias en la
   escuela
para que los conocimientos que
   alcancen les ayuden a enfrentarse
   al futuro con esperanza.

Bendice su cuestionamiento de
   la autoridad y la tradición.

Que su simpleza nos rete a todos
   a trabajar por la justicia y la
   paz mundial.

Bendice a sus familias y seres
   queridos
para que siempre puedan conocer
   la profundidad, alcance y
   poder de tu amor.

Te lo pedimos por Cristo
   nuestro Señor.

Amén.

Thomas Tomaszek
Oficina de Ministerio Juvenil
Diócesis de Milwaukee

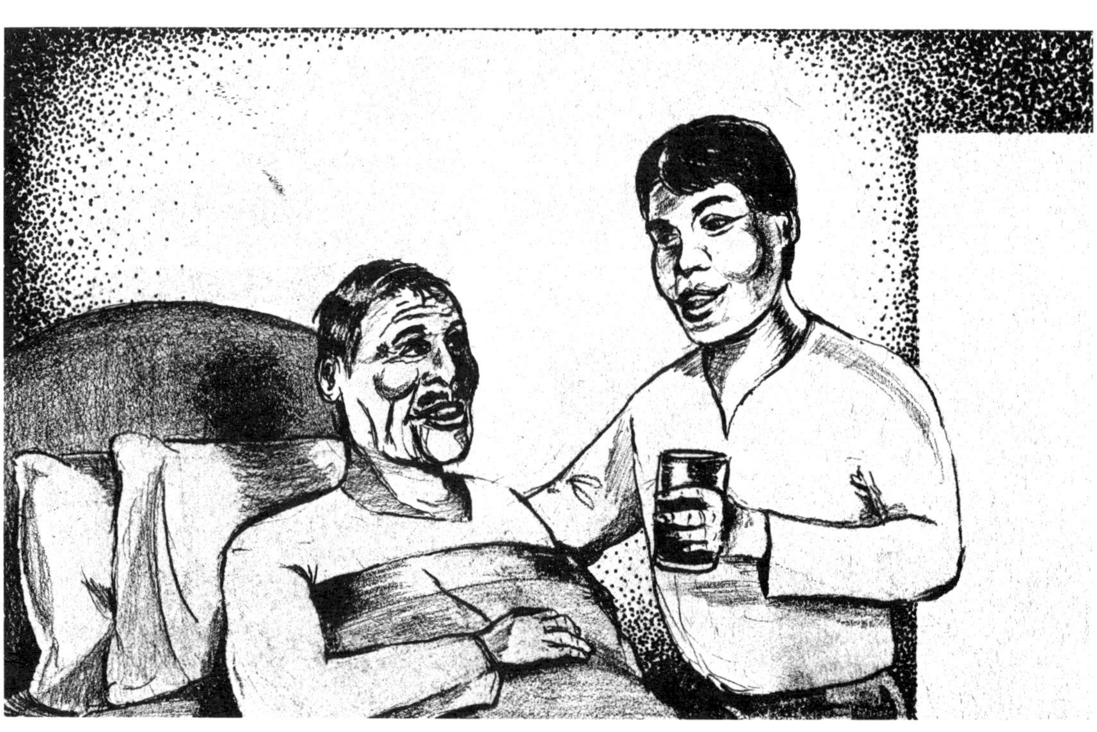

Servicio de Reconciliación

CANTO

Se puede seleccionar uno de los siguientes:

- *"Eres Amado por Dios"*
- *"Yo Te Amo Mucho"*
- *"Amémonos de Corazón"*

INTRODUCCIÓN

Comentador:

Estamos aquí para ponernos en la Presencia de la Misericordia de Dios y ver quién somos. Somos personas con diversos dones que Dios ha puesto en cada uno de nosotros. Esos dones son: amor, perdón, aceptación, y sobre todo, reconciliación. Volver a la LUZ para brillar de nuevo. La reconciliación es sanar y volver a juntar lo que debe estar unido: DIOS Y NOSOTROS. No siempre somos la persona que queremos ser. No siempre somos la persona que deberíamos ser. Pero, definitivamente, somos personas amadas por Dios. El Sacramento de la Reconciliación nos recuerda la dignidad de las personas. Cuando perdonamos a los demás respetamos esa dignidad. ¿Cuántas veces? Jesús dijo: "Setenta veces siete." Tantas veces cuanto diga la persona que está arrepentida, hay que salir a su encuentro, sanar, perdonar y dar LUZ. De esta manera imitamos a Jesús que salió al encuentro, sanó, perdonó, y dijo: YO SOY LA LUZ DEL MUNDO.

LECTURA

Lucas 15:11-32: El Hijo Pródigo

Todos:

Esta es la Palabra de Dios.

Comentador:

¿Cómo perdonó Dios? ¿Cuál es Su actitud ante el que se siente fracasado, dolido, enfermo y muerto por el pecado? Jesús mismo nos contó cómo Dios perdona. Ya lo escuchamos en su PALABRA ahora vamos a presenciarlo en una dramatización.

DRAMATIZACIÓN

Se puede narrar y dramatizar la parábola del Hijo Pródigo. Se necesitan 5 jóvenes.

MOMENTOS DE REFLEXIÓN

En estos momentos todos tienen una vela que se les ha dado anteriormente que se va encendiendo del Cirio Pascual que está en el centro y se pasan unos a otros la LUZ de CRISTO. Se tiene música de fondo suave y todo obscuro excepto las velas encendidas.

Comentador:

¿Qué me dice Cristo a mí en este momento?

LETANÍA

Lector(es): (se pueden seleccionar varios jóvenes para que cada uno lea las diferentes peticiones)

- Por las veces que no hemos amado y no nos hemos dejado amar,

Respuesta:
Señor, ten piedad de nosotros.

- Por las veces que no hemos sido LUZ para otros, **R/.**

- Por las veces que nos hemos hechos sordos a las necesidades de los demás, **R/.**

- Por las veces que no hemos seguido los valores de Jesús **R/.**

- Por las veces que no hemos perdonado o aceptado a los demás cómo Jesús nos pide **R/.**

- Por las veces que nos hemos dejado llevar por el ruido del mundo sin pensar en el silencio de Dios y su posible LLAMADO a su servicio **R/.**

- Por las veces que hemos sido pasivos en los momentos que cuenta mucho nuestra VOZ para causar cambio para mejorar el mundo **R/.**

ORACIÓN

Tómanos como somos Señor, transfórmanos como quieres que seamos y ayúdanos a vivir tus valores en el mundo de quien tú fuiste víctima.

Todos:

Amén.

ACTIVIDAD

Comentador:

Ahora recordemos un momento en nuestras vidas que hemos estado en la obscuridad o recordemos aquello que me impide que llegue Cristo a mí...Escríbelo en el papelito y luego apaga tu vela.

[El salón se quedará completamente obscuro, con excepción del Cirio Pascual y una cruz grande en el suelo delante de la luz con clavos y martillo.]

El pecado es como la obscuridad. Cuando pecamos estamos diseminando la obscuridad por todo el mundo. Cuando hacemos algo bueno, estamos diseminando la LUZ DE CRISTO. Cristo murió en la CRUZ para darnos la LUZ. Él tomó para sí todos los pecados del mundo. Con la vela y el papelito donde están escritos los pecados, cuando estén listos cada uno puede levantarse para clavar sus pecados en la cruz diciendo:

Cordero de Dios, que quitas los pecados del mundo.

Todos respondemos:

Ten piedad de nosotros.

[Si hay sacerdotes se puede dar la oportunidad de la Confesión. Después de la confesión cada joven enciende la vela con el Cirio Pascual y vuelve a su lugar.]

Comentador:

Pasamos de la muerte a la vida. De la obscuridad a la LUZ. Somos Hijos de la Luz.

[Cuando todos ya estén en su lugar con las velitas encendidas se canta esta canción: "Mi Pequeñita Luz, la Dejaré Brillar".]

EL ABRAZO DE PAZ

Comentador:

Vamos unos a otros diciéndonos: Cristo te perdonó y yo también. Tenemos la necesidad de oir que somos perdonados y también la necesidad de recibir el abrazo de aceptación.

ORACIÓN FINAL

Somos tus hijos. Somos la Luz que lleva la esperanza de formar el Reino de Dios que es el reino de Paz, Justicia y Amor. Somos enviados a hacer lo que Dios ha hecho con nosotros. Con la ayuda de Dios Padre, Hijo y Espíritu Santo, vayamos a cumplir su mandato.

Todos:

Amén.

CANTO

"Estamos de Fiesta Con Jesús"

Hna. Ninfa Garza, MJ
Diócesis de Brownsville

Arte Reproducible

El arte en esta sección ha sido creado para que se pueda usar en boletines, invitaciones, estandartes, afiches, camisetas, o en la manera en que su parroquia, escuela o com- unidad lo desee. Puede calcar, fotocopiar, ampliar o reducir el arte que inclumimos en esta sección y en este libro para que su celebración del Día Mundial de la Juventud de 1992 sea un triunfo.

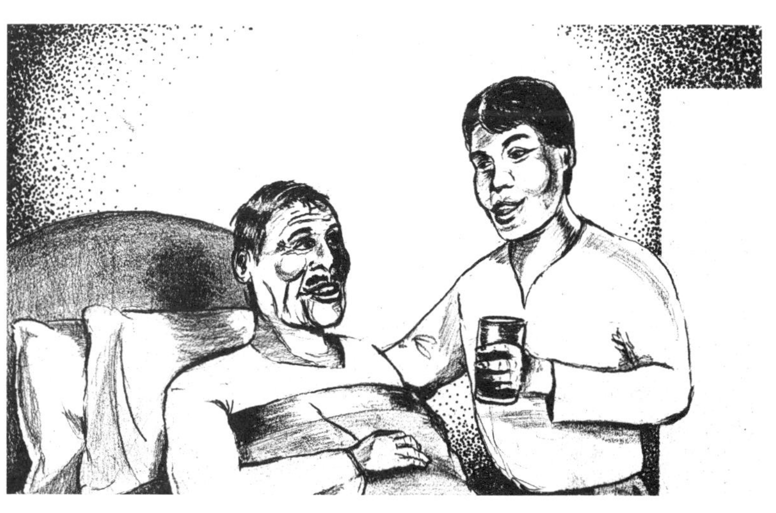

Día Mundial de la Juventud de 1992 ¡Vive la Fe Comparte la Historia!

Día Mundial de la Juventud de 1992 ¡Vive la Fe Comparte la Historia!

Día Mundial de la Juventud de 1992 ¡Vive la Fe Comparte la Historia!

Día Mundial de la Juventud de 1992 ¡Vive la Fe Comparte la Historia!